THE NEW CHEMICAL LIGHT

MICHAEL SENDIVOGIUS

Published and Distributed by:

Angelnook Publishing, Inc.
1277 Cranston Street
Cranston, RI 02920
www.angelnookpublishing.com

Copyright © 2011 Angelnook Publishing, Inc.

No part of this book may be reproduced in any form or by any electronic or mechanical means including information storage and retrieval systems without the express written consent of Angelnook Publishing, Inc.

All rights reserved.

ISBN: 1468115227
ISBN-13: 978-1468115222

ABOUT THE COVER ARTIST

JP Madison spends the majority of her time communicating with the Archangelic realm and Universal community. Through this divine unity Ms. Madison relates original, unedited inscriptions and artistic impressions.

Intending to intrigue, Ms. Madison suggests the viewer travel her path and unravel the mystical messages within her publications. Her comprehensive research and archived information is intended to target Indigo and Crystal children that can make a difference to tomorrow's society.

Currently Madison resides in New England. She has primarily worked in the financial sector having no formal training as an artist. Her passions and heartfelt appreciation are exhibited in all aspects of her personal and professional guided missions signifying the limitless possibilities that can transpire from divine inspiration.

THE
NEW CHEMICAL LIGHT

DRAWN FROM THE FOUNTAIN OF NATURE AND FROM MANUAL EXPERIENCE

TO WHICH IS ADDED

A TREATISE CONCERNING SULPHUR

[THE AUTHOR'S ANAGRAM]:

"DIVI LESCHI GENUS AMO"

IN THIS SENTENCE: "I LOVE THE DIVINE RACE OF LESCHI," ALL THE LETTERS OF THE AUTHOR'S NAME ARE FOUND TRANSPOSED, --- TO WIT:

MICHAEL SENDIVOGIUS.

CONTENTS

PREFACE	I
SIMPLICITY IS THE SEAL OF TRUTH	1
THE FRIST TREATISE	3
SECOND TREATISE	7
THIRD TREATISE	11
FOURTH TREATISE	13
FIFTH TRACT	17
SIXTH TREATISE	19
SEVENTH TREATISE	23
EIGHTH TREATISE	27
NINTH TREATISE	29
TENTH TREATISE	31
ELEVENTH TREATISE	33
TWELFTH TREATISE	39
EPILOGUE	41
A PREFACE TO THE RIDDLE OF THE SAGES	47
A PARABLE, OR ENIGMA OF THE SAGES	51
A DIALOGUE BETWEEN MERCURY, THE ALCHEMISTS, AND NATURE	57

CONTENTS

CONCERNING SULPHUR PREFACE	77
CONCERNING SULPHUR	81
CONCERNING ELEMENTARY EARTH	83
CONCERNING ELEMENTARY WATER	85
CONCERNING ELEMENTARY AIR	91
CONCERNING ELEMENTARY FIRE	93
CONCERNING THE THREE PRINCIPLES OF ALL THINGS	101
CONCERNING SULPHUR	109

PREFACE

UPON ALL GENUINE SEEKERS OF THE GREAT CHEMICAL ART, OR SONS OF HERMES, THE AUTHOR IMPLORES THE DIVINE BLESSING AND SALVATIONS.

When I considered in my mind the great number of deceitful books and forged Alchemistic "receipts", which have been put in circulation by heartless impostors, though they do not contain even a spark of truth --- and how many persons have been and are still daily led astray by them? -- it occurred to me that I could not do better than communicate the Talent committed to me by the Father of Lights to the Sons and Heirs of Knowledge. I also wish to let posterity see that in our own age, as well as in ancient times, this singularly gracious philosophical Blessing has not been denied to a few favoured men. For certain reasons I do not think it advisable to publish my name; chiefly, because I do not seek for praise for myself, but am only anxious to assist the lovers of philosophy. The vainglorious desire for fame I leave to those who are content to seem what they, in reality, are not. The facts and deductions which I have here briefly set down are transcribed from that manual --- experience, graciously bestowed upon me by the Most High; and my object is to enable those who have laid a sound foundation in the elementary part of this most noble Art, to advance to a more satisfying fullness of knowledge, and to put them on their guard against those depraved "vendors of smoke," who delight in fraud and imposition. Our science is not a dream, as the vulgar crowd imagines, or the empty invention of idle men, as the foolish suppose. It is the very truth of philosophy itself, which the voice of conscience and of love bid me conceal no longer. In these wicked days, indeed, when virtue and vice are accounted alike, the ingratitude and unbelief of men keep our Art from appearing openly before the public gaze. Yet this glorious truth is even now capable of being apprehended by learned and unlearned persons of virtuous lives, and there are many persons of all nations now living who have beheld Diana unveiled. But as many, either from ignorance or from a desire to conceal their knowledge, are daily teaching and inducing others to believe that the soul of gold can be extracted, and then imparted to other substances; and thereby entice numbers to incur great waste of time, labour, and money: let the sons of Hermes know for certain that the extracting of the essence of gold is a mere fond delusion, as those who persist in it will be taught to their cost by experience, the only arbitress from whose judgment seat there is no appeal. If, on the other hand, a person is able to transmute the smallest piece of metal (with or without gain) into genuine gold or silver which abides all the usual tests, he may justly be said to have opened the gates of Nature, and cleared the way for profounder and more advanced study. It is with this object that I dedicate the following pages, which embody the results of my experience, to the sons of knowledge, that by a careful study of the working of Nature they may be enabled to lift the veil, and enter her inmost sanctuary. To this final goal of our sacred philosophy they must travel by the royal road which Nature herself has marked out for them. Let me therefore admonish the gentle reader that my meaning is to be apprehended not so much from the outward husk of my words, as from the inward spirit of Nature. If this warning is neglected, he may spend his time, labour, and money in vain. Let him consider that this mystery is for wise men, and not for fools. The inward meaning of our philosophy will be unintelligible to vainglorious boasters, to conceited mockers, and to men who smother the clamorous voice of conscience with the insolence of a wicked life; as also to those ignorant persons who have fondly staked their happiness on albefactions and rubrefactions and other equally senseless methods. The right understanding of our Art is by the gift of God, or by the ocular demonstration of a teacher, and can be attained only by diligent, humble search, and prayerful dependence on the Giver of all good things; now, God rejects those who do hate Him and scorn knowledge. In conclusion, I would earnestly ask the sons of knowledge to accept this Book in the spirit in which it was written; and when the HIDDEN has become MANIFEST to them and the inner gates of secret knowledge are flung open not to reveal this mastery to any unworthy person; also to remember their duty towards their suffering and distressed neighbours to avoid any ostentatious display of their power; and above all, to render to God, the Three in One, sincere and grateful thanks with their lips, in the silence of their hearts, and by refraining from any abuse of the Gift.

SIMPLICITY IS THE SEAL OF TRUTH

As after the completion of the preface it was found that it did not cover the whole of the space allotted to it, I have, at the publisher's request, there set down the "last will and testament of Arnold Villanovanus" which I once turned into Latin verse. I am conscious that the style of my versification is wanting in neatness and elegance; but this defect was partly caused by the necessity of adhering strictly and faithfully to the Author's meaning. Testament of Arnold de Villanova.

It is said that Arnold de Villanova a man who was as a credit to his race, signified his last will in the following words:

> It has its birth in the earth, its strength it doth acquire in the fire, and there becomes the true Stone of the ancient Sages. Let it be nourished for twice six hours with a clear liquid until its limbs begin to expand and grow apace. Then let it be placed in a dry and moderately warm spot for another period of twelve hours, until it has purged itself by giving out a thick steam or vapour, and

becomes solid and hard within. The 'virgin's milk' that is expressed from the better part of the Stone is then preserved in a carefully closed oval-shaped distilling vessel of glass, and is day by day wondrously changed by the quickening fire, until all the different colours resolve themselves into a fixed gentle splendour of a white radiance, which soon, under the continued genial influence of the fire, changes to a glorious purple, the outward and visible sign of the final perfection of your work.

THE FIRST TREATISE

OF NATURE, WHAT SHE IS, AND WHAT MANNER OF MEN HER DISCIPLES OUGHT TO BE

Many Sages, Scholars, and learned men have in all ages, and (according to Hermes) even so early as the days before the Flood, written much concerning the preparation of the Philosopher's Stone; and if their books could be understood without a knowledge of the living processes of Nature, one might almost say that they are calculated to supersede the study of the real world around us. But though they never departed from the simple ways of Nature they have something to teach us, which, in these more sophisticated times, still need to learn, because we have applied ourselves to what are regarded as the more advanced branches of knowledge, and despise the study of so "simple " a thing as natural Generation. Hence we pay more heed to impossible things than to those objects which are broadly exhibited before our very eyes, we excel more in subtle speculations than in a sober study of Nature, and of the meaning of the Sages. It is one of the most remarkable features of human nature that we neglect those things which seem familiar, and are eager for new and strange information. The workman who has attained the highest degree of excellence in his Art, neglects it, and applies himself to something else, or else abuses his knowledge. Our longing for an increase of knowledge urges us ever onward towards some final goal, in which we imagine that we shall find full rest and satisfaction, like the ant which is not endowed with wings till the last days of its life. In our time, the Philosophical Art has become a very subtle matter; it is the craft of the goldsmith compared with that of the humble workman who exercises his calling at the forge. We have made such mighty strides in advance that if the ancient Masters of our science, Hermes and Geber and Raymond Lullius, were to rise from the dead, they would be treated by our modern Alchemists not as Sages but as only humble learners. They would seem very poor scholars in our modern lore of futile distillations, circulations, calcinations and in all the other countless operations wherewith modern research has so famously enriched our Art though without understanding the sense of the ancient writings. In all these respects, our learning is vastly superior to theirs. Only one thing is unfortunately wanting to us which they possessed, namely, the knack they had of actually preparing the Philosopher's Stone. Perhaps, then, their simple methods were after all the best; and it is on this supposition that I desire, in this volume, to teach you to understand Nature so that our vain imaginations may not misdirect us in the true and simple way. Nature then, is one, true, simple, self-contained, created by God and informed with a certain universal spirit. Its end and origin are God. Its unity is also found in God, because God made all things. Nature is the one source of all things: nor is anything in the world outside Nature, or contrary to Nature. Nature is divided into four "places" in which she brings forth all things that appear and that are in the shade; and according to the good or bad quality of the "place" she brings forth good or bad things. There are only four qualities which are in all things and yet do not agree among themselves, as one is always striving to obtain the mastery over the rest. Nature is not visible, though she acts visibly; she is a volatile spirit who manifests herself in material shapes, and her existence is in the Will of God. Students of Nature should be such as is Nature herself --- true, simple, patient, constant, and so on; above all, they should fear God, and love their neighbors. They should always be ready to learn from Nature and to be guided by her methods, ascertaining by visible and sensible examples whether that which they propose to perform is in accordance with her possibilities. If we would reproduce something already accomplished by Nature, we follow her, but if we would improve on her performance, we must know in and by what it is ameliorated. For instance, if we desire to impart to a metal greater excellence than Nature has given to it, we must take the metallic substance both in its male and its female varieties, else all our efforts will be in vain. It is as impossible to produce a metal out of a plant, It is most important for us to know her "places" and those which are most in harmony and most closely allied, in order that we may join things together according to Nature, and not attempt to confound vegetables with animals, or animals with metals. Everything should be made to act on that which is like to it --- and then Nature will perform her duty, as to make a tree out of a dog or any other animal.

SECOND TREATISE

CONCERNING THE OPERATION OF NATURE IN OUR SUBSTANCE, AND ITS SEED

I have already said that Nature is one, true, and consistent, and that she is known by her products, such as trees, herbs, &c. I have also described the qualifications of a student of Nature. Now I will say a few words about the operation of Nature. As Nature has her being in the Will of God, so her will, or seed is in the Elements. She is one, and produces different things but only through the mediate instrumentality of seed. For Nature performs whatsoever the sperm requires of her, and is, as it were only the instrument of some artisan. The seed if anything is more useful to the artist than Nature herself; for Nature: for Nature without seed is, what a goldsmith is without silver and gold, or a husbandman without seed corn. Wherever there is seed, Nature will work through it, whether it be good or bad. Nature works on "seed" as God works on the free will of man. Truly it is a great marvel to behold Nature obeying the seed not because she is forced to do so but of her own will. In like manner, God permits man to do what he pleases not because He is constrained but of His good and free bounty. The seed, then, is the elixir or of anything, or its quintessence, or its most perfect digestion and decoction, or, again, the Balm of Sulphur, which is the same as the radical moisture in metals. We might say much more about this seed, but can only mention those facts which are of importance in our Art. The four elements produce seed, through the will of God and the imagination of Nature; and as the seed of the male animal has its centre or storing place in the kidneys, so the four elements by their continual action project a constant supply of seed to the centre of the earth, where it is digested, and whence it proceeds again in generative motions. Now the centre of the earth is a certain void place wherein nothing is at rest; and upon the margin or circumference of this centre the four elements project their qualities. As the male seed is emitted into the womb of the female, where only so much as is needed is retained while the rest is driven out again, so the magnetic force of our earth-centre attracts to itself as much as is needed of the cognate seminal substance, while that which cannot be used for vital generation is thrust forth in the shape of stones and other rubbish. This is the fountain-head of all things terrestrial. Let us illustrate the matter by supposing a glass of water to be set in the middle of a table, round the margin of which are placed little heaps of salt, and of powders of different colours. If the water be poured out, it will run all over the table in divergent rivulets, and will become salt where it touches the salt, red where it dissolves the red powder, and so on. The water does not change the "places," but the several places differentiate the water. In the same way, the seed which is the product of the four elements is projected in all directions from the earth-centre, and produces different things, according to the quality of the different places. Thus, while the seed of all things is one, it is made to generate a great variety of things, just as the seed of a man might produce a man if projected into the womb of a female of his own species, or a monstrous variety of abortions, if projected into the wombs of different female animals. So long as Nature's seed remains in the centre it can indifferently produce a tree or a metal, a herb or a stone, and in like manner according to the purity of the place, it will produce what is less or more pure. But how do the elements generate the sperm or seed ? There are four elements, two heavy and two light, two dry and two moist, but one driest and one moistest of all; and these are male and female. By God's will each of these is constantly striving to produce things like to itself in its own sphere. Moreover they are constantly acting on one another, and the subtle essences of all are combined in the centre, where they are well mixed and sent forth again by Archeus, the servant of Nature, as is more fully set forth in the Epilogue of these twelve Treatises.

THIRD TREATISE

CONCERNING THE TRUE AND FIRST MATTER OF METALS

The first matter of metals is twofold, and one without the other cannot create a metal. The first and principal substance is the moisture of air mingled with warmth. This substance the Sages have called Mercury, and in the philosophical sea it is governed by the rays of the Sun and the Moon. The second substance is the dry heat of the earth, which is called Sulphur. But as this substance has always been kept a great mystery, let us declare it more fully, and especially its weight, ignorance of which mars the whole work. The right substance, if the quantity of it which is taken be wrong, can produce nothing but an abortion. There are some who take the entire body for their matter, that is, for their seed or sperm; others take only a part of it: both are on the wrong track. If any one, for instance, were to attempt the creation of a man out of a man's hand and a woman's foot, he would fail. For there is in every body a central atom, or vital point of the seed (its 1/8200 part), even in a grain of wheat. Neither the body nor the grain is all seed, but every body has a small seminal spark, which the other parts protect from all excess of heat and cold. If you have ears and eyes treasure up this fact, and be on your guard against those who would use the whole grain as seed, and those who strive to produce a highly rarefied metallic substance by the vain solution and mixture of different metals. For even the purest metals contain a certain element of impurity, while in the inferior the proportion is greater. You will have all you want if you find the point of Nature, which you must not, however, look for in the vulgar metals; it is not to be found therein, for all these, and common gold more especially, are dead. But the metals which we advise you to take are living and have vital spirits. Fire is the life of metals while they are still in their ore, and the fire of smelting is their death. But the first matter of metals as a certain moisture mixed with warm air. Its appearance is that of oily water adhering to all pure and impure things; yet in some places it is found more abundantly than in others because the earth is more open and porous in one place than in another, and has a greater magnetic force. When it becomes manifest, it is clothed in a certain vesture, especially in places where it has nothing to cling to. It is known by the fact that it is composed of three principles; but, as a metallic substance it is only one without any visible sign of conjunction, except that which may be called its vesture or shadow namely, sulphur, &c.

FOURTH TREATISE

HOW METALS ARE PRODUCED IN THE BOWELS IN THE EARTH

The metals are produced in this way: after the four elements have projected their power and virtues to the centre of the earth, they are, in the hands of the Archeus of Nature distilled and sublimed by the heat of perpetual motion towards the surface of the earth. For the earth is porous, and the air by distillation through the pores of the earth is resolved into a water out of which all things are generated. You should know that the seed of metals is the same, in the first instance, as the sperm of all other things, viz., a vaporous moisture. Hence it is foolish to seek the dissolution of metals in the first matter, which is nothing but a vapour, and in so doing philosophers have not comprehended the first matter, but only the second, as Bernard Trevisan well argues, though in a somewhat obscure manner, for he addressed himself to the Sons of the Doctrine. For my part before openly explaining this theory, I would warn all men not to seek that which exists everywhere by itself in a soft volatile form by so many circulations, calcinations, and reiterations of hard gold and silver, which can never be changed back into their original substance. Let us follow the real meaning of the writers of Alchemy whose works we read, and remember that if Art would produce any solid and permanent effect, it must follow in the footsteps of Nature, and be guided by her methods. It must trust itself to the guidance of Nature as far as Nature will lead, and go beyond her by still adhering to her rules. Now I said that all things are produced of a liquid air or a vapour which the elements distil into the centre of the earth by a continual motion, and that as soon as the Archeus has received it, his wisdom sublimes it through the pores, and distributes it to each place, producing different things according to the diverse places in which it is deposited. Some think that each metal has its own seed. But this is a great mistake for there is only one Seed. The sperm which appears in Saturn is the same as that which is found in gold, silver, copper, &c.; their difference is caused by the place, and by the time during which Nature was at work upon them, the procreation of silver being achieved sooner than that of gold, and so with the other metals. The vapour which is sublimed by heat from the centre of the earth, passes either through cold or warm places. If the place be warm and pure, and contain adhering to it a certain fatness of sulphur, the vapour (or Mercury of the Sages) joins itself to its fatness, and sublimes it together with itself. If in the course of its further sublimation this unctuous vapour reaches other places where the earth has already been subtilized, purified, and rendered moist by previous ascending vapours, it fills the pores of this earth, and with it becomes gold. But if this unctuous moisture be carried to impure and cold places, it becomes lead; if the earth be pure and mingled with sulphur, it becomes copper. For the purer the place is, the more beautiful and perfect will the metal be. We must also note that the vapour is constantly ascending, and in its ascent from the earth's centre to its superficies, it purifies the places through which it passes. Hence precious metals are found now where none existed a thousand years ago, for this vapour, by its continual progress, ever subtilizes the crude and impure, and as continually carries away the pure with itself. This is the circulation and reiteration of Nature. All places are being more and more purified: and the purer they become the nobler are their products. In the winter this unctuous vapor is congealed by the frost. At the return of spring it is set free, and is the Magnesia which attracts to itself the kindred Mercury of the air, and gives life to all things through the rays of the Sun, the Moon and the Stars, thus bringing forth grass, flowers, and the like, for Nature is never idle Even during a single moment. This then, is the only true account of the generation of Metals. The earth is purged by a long distillation, and when the unctuous or fatty vapour approaches, the same are procreated, nor are they ever otherwise begotten notwithstanding the imaginations of those who misinterpret on this point the writings of the philosophers.

FIFTH TRACT

ON THE GENERATION OF ALL KINDS OF STONES

The substance of stones is the same as that of all other things; and their quality is determined by the purity of the places in which they arise when the four elements distil their vapour to the centre of the earth, the Archeus of Nature expels and sublimes it in such a manner that it carries with it in its passage through the pores of the earth, all the impurities of these places up to the surface, where they are congealed by the air, all that pure air engenders being congealed by crude air, their ingression being mutual, so that they join one with another, since Nature rejoices in Nature. Thus rocks and stones are gradually built up and generated. Now the larger the pores of the earth, the greater is the quantity of impurities carried upward; and thus the earth is most completely purified under those places where there is a great accumulation of stones or rocks at the surface, and in this manner the procreation of metals becomes easier in these places. This explains the fact that metals are scarcely ever found in plains, but nearly always in the bowels of rocky hills. The plains are often moist with elemental water which attracts to itself the rising vapour, and with it is digested by the rays of the Sun into the rich clay which potters use. In places where the soil is gross, and the vapour contains neither unctuousness nor sulphur, it produces herbs and grass in the meadows. The precious stones, such as diamonds, rubies, and emeralds, chrysopras, onyx, and carbuncle, are all generated in the same manner as ordinary stones. When the natural vapour is sublimed by itself without sulphur or the unctuosity of which we have spoken and reaches a place where there is pure salt water (i.e., in very cold places, where our sulphur cannot exist, for could it exist, this effect would be hindered), diamonds are formed. The unctuous sulphur which rises with the vapour cannot move without warmth and is instantly congealed. When it reaches a slightly cold place, leaving the vapour to continue its upward movement without it. Colours are imparted to precious stones in this way. When the unctuous sulphur is congealed by the perpetual motion, the spirit of the water digests it in passing and purifies it by the water of the salt, until it assumes a red or white colour. This colour is volatilized by so many repeated distillations, and at length is borne upward with the purifying vapour, which by its aid is able to enter imperfect bodies, and thus to pervade them with colour; the colour is united to the partly congealed water and fills all its pores so that the two are absolutely one. For water which has no spirit is congealed by heat, and water which has a spirit is congealed by cold; but he who knows how to congeal water by means of heat, and to join to it a spirit, is like to discover something a thousand times more precious than gold, or anything which is in the world. Let him separate the spirit from the waters in order that it may putrefy, and that the grain may appear. Then let him purge off the dross, and reduce the spirit to water. This union will produce a branch which bears little resemblance to the parent stem.

SIXTH TREATISE

CONCERNING THE SECOND MATTER AND PUTREFACTION

We have spoken of the first matter of all things, and after what manner they are born by Nature without seed, that is, after what manner Nature receives the matter from the elements whereof she engenders seed. We will now consider this seed and the things evolved from it. Everything that has seed is multiplied thereby, but not without the aid of Nature for seed is nothing but congealed air, or a vaporous humour enclosed in a body; and unless it be dissolved by a warm vapour, it cannot work. Now, the nature of this seed which is produced out of the four elements, is threefold: it is either Mineral, or Vegetable, or Animal. Mineral seed is known only to the Sages. Vegetable seed is common and vulgar, as we see in fruits. Animal seed is known by imagination. But vegetable seed exhibits most clearly the process by which Nature evolves natural objects out of the four elements. Winter is the cause of putrefaction: it congeals the vital spirit in trees, and when the heat of the Sun, which magnetically attracts moisture, sets it free, the natural heat (of the tree) which is thereby stirred up, drives a subtle vapour of water towards the surface, and makes the sap to flow, always separating the pure from the impure, though the impure may sometimes precede the pure. That which is pure is congealed into flowers, the impure becomes leaves, the gross and thick hardens into bark. The bark of the tree remains fixed; the leaves fall when the pores are obstructed by heat or cold; the flowers receive a colour according to the quality of the natural heat, and bear fruit or seed. We may instance the apple, wherein is the sperm, whence the tree does not spring; but in this sperm is the seed or grain interiorly, whence the tree is born even without sperm, for multiplication is not of the sperm but of the seed. Thus we see how Nature, without our help, creates vegetable seed out of the four elements. But how about Minerals? Nature brings forth Mineral or Metallic seed in the bowels of the earth. This is the reason why so many will not believe in its existence -- because it is invisible. And on this account the vulgar unbelief is not so greatly to be wondered at: for if they hardly understand that which is openly before their eyes, how should they know anything about that which they cannot see. Yet, whether they believe it or not, the fact remains the same, and it is most true that which is above is as that which is below, and that which is born above has origin from the same source which is at work down below, even in the bowels of the earth. What prerogative have vegetables above metals that God should give seed to the one and withhold it from the other? Are not metals as much in His sight as trees? It is certain that nothing can grow without seed; for that which has no seed, is dead. The four elements must either bring forth metallic seed or produce metals without seed. In the latter case, they cannot be perfect: for nothing is complete without seed. He who can bring himself to believe that metals are destitute of seed, is unworthy to understand the mysteries of our Art. The metals then really contain their own proper seed; and it is generated in the following way. The vapour which (in the manner repeatedly described rises from the earth's centre, and is called Mercury not on account of its essence but on account of its fluidity, and the facility with which it adheres to anything, is assimilated to the sulphur on account of its internal heat; and, after congelation, is the radical humour. Thus metals are indeed generated out of mercury; but those ignorant persons who say that this first substance of metals is ordinary mercury, confound the whole hole body with the seed that is in it, seeing that common mercury, too, contains metallic seed, as well as the other metals. Let us illustrate the matter by the analogy of the human body. Therein it is certain that there is a seed whereby the species of mankind is propagated. That body (which may be likened to common mercury) contains seed, which is not seen, and of which the quantity is very small in proportion to the size of the whole body: the process of generation is performed not by the whole body, but by this seminal "congealed watery vapour." But as no vital generation could take place if the body were dissected in order to get at the seed, as the murdering of the body would kill the seed -- so ignorant Alchemists may be said to murder the body and kill the seed of metals, when they dissolve their bodies, whether of gold, silver, or lead, and corrode them with aqua fortis, in order to obtain the metallic seed. All multiplication is performed by means of male and female seed; and the two (which by themselves are barren) must be conjoined in order to bring forth fruit, i.e., a new form. Whosoever, therefore, would bring forth any good thing must take the sperm or the seed, and not the entire body. Take, then, the living male and the living female, and join them in order that they may project a sperm for the procreation of a fruit according to their kind, for let no one presume to suppose that he can make the first matter. The first matter of man is earth, and there is no one so bold as to dream that he can create a man. God alone can perform this artifice. But if the second substance (or seed) which is already created, be put in the proper place, Nature will produce a new form of the same species. The Artist only separates what is subtle from its grosser elements, and puts it into the proper "vessel." Nature does the rest. As a thing begins, so it ends. Out of one arise two, and out of two one -- as of God the Father there was begotten God the Son, and from the two proceeded God the Holy Ghost. Thus was the world made, and so also shall it end. Consider carefully these few points, and you will find, firstly the Father, then the Father and the Son, lastly, the Holy Spirit. You will find the four elements, the four luminaries, the two celestials, the two centrics. In a word there is nothing, has been, and shall be nothing in the World which is otherwise than it appears in this symbol, and a volume might be filled with its mysteries. I say, therefore, it is the attribute of God alone to make one out of one, you must produce one thing out of two by natural generation. Know, then, that the multiplying sperm is the second substance, and not the first. For the first substance of things is not seen, but is hidden in Nature or the elements: the second substance is occasionally seen by the children of knowledge.

SEVENTH TREATISE

CONCERNING THE VIRTUE OF THE SECOND MATTER

But in order that you may the better know this second matter, I will describe to you its virtues. Nature is divided into three kingdoms, the mineral, the vegetable, and the animal. It is manifest that the mineral kingdom could subsist of itself were there no vegetables or animals in the world; the vegetable in like manner, is independent of the animal and mineral. These two kingdoms were created in independence. The animal kingdom alone depends for its subsistence on the two others, and is the most noble and excellent of all; and seeing that it is the last of the three, it governs the two others, because virtue expends itself at the third, even as it is multiplied in the second. In the vegetable kingdom the first substance is the herb or the tree, which you cannot create, but which is produced by Nature alone. The second substance is the seed which you see, by which herbs and trees are propagated. In the animal kingdom the first substance is the beast or man, whom you cannot create; but the seed, or second substance, by which they are propagated, you know. In the mineral kingdom, too, you are unable to create a metal, and if you boast that you can do so, Nature will laugh at your pretensions; given even the possession of that first matter which is vaunted by the philosophers, namely, the centric salt, you cannot multiple it without gold; but the vegetable seed of metals is known only to the Sons of Science. In the case of plants, the seed is seen outwardly, and is digested by warm air. In animals the seed appears inwardly and outwardly, and is prepared in the kidneys of the male. Water is the seed of minerals, in the very centre of their heart and life; and the "kidneys of its digestion" are fire. The receptacle of vegetable seed is the earth; the receptacle of animal seed the womb of the female; and air is the receptacle of water -- the mineral seed. The receptacles of seed are the same as congelations of bodies; digestion is the same as solution, and putrefaction the same as destruction. The specific property of seed is to enter into union with other substances belonging to the same kingdom, because it is subtle, and, in fact, air congealed by fatness into water. It is recognizable by the fact that it does not become naturally united to anything outside the kingdom to which it belongs. It is not dissolved, but only congealed, as it does not need solution but only congelation. Hence it is necessary that the pores of bodies be opened to admit the sperm, in the centre of which lies the seed (which is air). When it enters its proper womb it is congealed, and congeals the pure or mixed substance which it finds. So long as there is any seed in the body the body lives; when it is all consumed the body dies; and any emission of seed weakens the body, as may be seen in the case of dissolute persons, and of trees which have been too richly laden with fruit. The seed, then, is invisible, but the sperm can be seen, and is even as a living soul, which is not found in dead things. It is extracted after two manners, of which the first is gentle and the second violent. Nothing is produced without seed, but everything comes into being by means of seed. Let all sons of knowledge remember that seed is vainly sought in dry trees, and that it is found only in those which are green.

EIGHTH TREATISE

HOW NATURE OPERATES THROUGH OUR ART IN THE SEED

Seed in itself produces no fruit, if it be not placed by Nature or Art in its own proper womb. Though seed in itself is the most glorious of all created things, yet the womb is its life, which causes the putrefaction of the enclosing grain or sperm, brings about the congelation of the vital atom, nourishing and stimulating its growth by the warmth of its own body. All this is constantly and regularly being enacted (by months, years, and seasons) in the above said three natural kingdoms. The process can be hastened artificially in the vegetable and mineral, but not in the animal world. In the mineral kingdom, Art can do something which Nature is unable to perform, by removing the crude air which stops up the outward pores of minerals, not in the bowels of the earth but in the circumference. The elements vie in projecting their seed into the centre of the earth in order that it may there be digested. The centre, by a caloric movement, emits it into the womb; of these wombs there are an untold number -- as many as there are places, and one place always purer than another. Know that a pure womb will bring forth a pure form of its own species. For instance, as among animals there are wombs of women, cows, mares, bitches, so in the mineral world there are metals, stones, and salts. Now salts principally demand consideration, with their localities, according as they are less or more important.

NINTH TREATISE

ON THE COMMIXTION OF METALS, AND THE ELICITING OF THE METALLIC SEED

We have spoken hitherto of Nature, of Art, of bodies, sperm and seed. Let us now proceed to the practical enquiry, how metals should be mixed, and how they are mutually related. For as a woman is generated in the same womb, and out of the same seed as a man, and the only difference is in the degree of digestion, and the purity of the blood and salts, so silver is produced from the same seed, and in the same womb as gold; but the womb of the silver had more water, and, as it were less digested blood than that of gold, according to the times of the celestial moon. But if you would understand the sexual union of the metals and their manner of emitting and receiving seed look at the celestial bodies of the planets. You will see that Saturn is higher than all the rest, to whom Jupiter succeeds, then Mars, the Sun, Venus, Mercury, while the last place is occupied by the Moon. The virtues of the planets descend, but do not ascend; and so as experiences teaches us, Mars is easily converted into Venus, but not Venus into Mars, which has an inferior sphere. Also Jupiter may be quickly transmuted into Mercury, because Jupiter has a higher place; the one is second after the firmament, the other second after the earth. Saturn is the highest, the Moon lowest; the Sun combines with all, but is never ameliorated by its inferiors. There is a great correspondence between Saturn and the Moon, the Sun being medial between them; as also between Mercury and Jupiter, Mars and Venus, which all have the Sun as their centre. Most operators know how to transmute iron into copper, or Venus, without using gold, they also know how to change Jupiter into Mercury some can prepare the Moon (silver) out of Saturn; but if they could prepare gold by these changes, their secret would be worth knowing indeed. For this reason I repeat that it is important to know the mutual correspondence of metals, and their possibilities of union. There is one metal which has power to consume all others, for it is, so to speak, their water, and almost their mother, and is resisted only by the radical humour of gold and silver, and ameliorated by it. This metal is called Chalybs (steel). If gold is united to it eleven times, and emits its seed, it is weakened even unto death; but the Chalybs (steel) conceives and brings forth a son much nobler than the father; and when the seed of the son is placed in her womb it purifies it, and renders it a thousand times better fitted to produce excellent fruit. There is another Chalybs (steel) which is like this one, and created as a thing by itself by Nature. This steel is able, with its wonderful virtue, to elicit from the rays of the "sun" that which so many have sought, and which is the chief principle of our Art.

TENTH TREATISE

ON THE SUPERNATURAL GENERATION OF THE SON OF THE SUN

We have treated of those things which are produced by Nature and have been created by God, so that those who are searchers of this science man comprehend more easily the possibility of Nature, and the utmost limit of her powers. I now go on to speak about the method of preparing the Philosophers Stone. The Stone or Tincture is nothing other than gold digested to the highest degree. Common gold resembles a plant without seed; but when such a plant is matured, it produces seed-and so, when gold is ripened, it produces its seed, or the Tincture. If any one asks why gold and other metals do not commonly produce seed I answer because the crudity of the ore, which has not sufficient heat, prevents it from being matured. In some places pure gold is found which Nature has been striving to mature, but which has not attained to ripeness on account of the crudity of the air. An analogous case is that of the orange tree, which bears no fruit in northern latitudes, because it has not sufficient warmth, while in warmer countries it ripens the most delicious fruit, and a like result it is possible to produce in colder countries, by means of artificial heat. The same thing happens with metallic natures, and so gold may be made to produce seed, by a wise and judicious Artist who knows how to assist Nature. Should he act independently of Nature, he would err, for in this science, as in all others, we can do nothing but supplement Nature, nor can we otherwise aid her than through the agency of heat or fire. Now, in order that Nature may be enabled to work upon a congealed metallic substance, wherein the spirit does not appear, the body must be dissolved and its pores opened. Now there are two kinds of solution, the violent and the natural; and under the former head come all those methods of solution which are in vogue among the vulgar herd of modern Alchemists, and the same are cold and useless. Natural solution takes place when the pores of the body are gently opened in our water, so that the digested seed can be emitted and placed in its womb. Our water is a water which does not wet the hands; it is a heavenly water, and yet not rain water. The "Body" is gold, which gives out the seed. Our silver (not common silver) is that which conceives the seed of the gold. There it is digested by our continual fire, for seven or even ten months, until our water consumes three, and leaves one; and this is something twofold. Then it is nourished with the milk of earth, or the fatness of that which is formed in the breasts of the earth, and is regulated and conserved by the putrefaction of the surrounding substance. In this way that infant of the second generation is born. Now us advance from theory to practice.

ELEVENTH TREATISE

CONCERNING THE PRACTICAL PREPARATION OF OUR STONE OR TINCTURE BY MEANS OF OUR ART

Our discourse in preceding chapters has been enlarged by appropriate examples which well facilitate the understanding of the practice, which, in accordance with natural procedure, must be performed as follows: take eleven grains of our earth, by as many doses, one grain of our gold, and two grains of our silver. Here you should carefully bear in mind that common gold and silver are of no use for our purpose, as they are dead. Those which I ask you to take are the living metals. Expose them to the heat of our fire, and there will come out of them a dry liquid. The earth will first be dissolved into a water which is called Mercury of the Sages, and this water will dissolve the bodies of the gold and silver, and consume them, till only the tenth part with one part remains, which is the radical metallic humour. Then take the water of saltpetre from our earth, in which is a living river and a flowing wave. Let this water be clear, and pour on it the radical humour: expose the whole to the fire of putrefaction and generation, which is not the same as that of the first operation. Regulate the heat judiciously, until there appear colours like those of the Peacock's Tail, and then continue to apply this well-regulated heat until the colours resolve themselves into a pronounced green. Be not weary but continue till the rest of the colours have manifested. When you observe at the bottom ashes of a brown colour, while the water is almost red, you should open the vessel and dip a feather into it. With this feather smear a morsel of iron, and if it becomes tinged, pour into the vessel as much of a certain water (which we will describe hereafter) as there is of crude air which has entered in, and then again subject it to coction over the same fire, until it colours the feather again. Further than this my experience does not go. The water I have mentioned is the menstruum of the world from the sphere of the Moon and so carefully rectified that it has power to calcine the Sun. Herein have I desired to discourse everything to your understanding and if sometimes you will take my meaning rather than my words, you will find that I have revealed all, more especially as regards the first and second work. It remains for me to say a few words about the fire. In the first operation the fire should be of one degree and continuous and should pervade the whole substance with an even warmth. In the second operation we need a natural fire, which digests and fixes the substance. Behold, I say unto you the truth! I have unfolded the regimen of the fire if only you understand Nature. But it is needful also to speak a few words concerning the vessel, which ought to be such as is indicated by Nature; and two of these vessels suffice. In the first operation the vessel should be round; in the second it should be somewhat smaller; it should also be of glass in the form of a vial or egg. But, know, above all things, that fire employed by Nature is one and its differences are determined by differences of distance. The vessel of Nature is also one, but we use two in order to accelerate the development of our substance; its material is one, but consists of two substances. If you would produce anything, look at the things that are produced. If you cannot understand those which are continually before your eyes, it will go hardly with you when you seek to produce those which are as yet unseen. Remember that God alone can create; but He has permitted the Sage to make manifest things that are hidden and concealed according to the ministry of Nature. Consider I pray you the simple water of the clouds. Who would believe that it contains in itself all mundane objects, hard stones, salts, air, earth, and fire? What shall I say of the earth, which seems simple enough and, and contains water, fire, salts, air, and much besides? O, admirable Nature, who knowest by the means of water how to produce the wonderful fruits of earth, who dost give life to them and nourish them by means of air! Everything depends upon the faculty of seeing which we bring to the study of nature. Common eyes, for instance, discern that the sun is hot; the eyes of the Sage see that the sun itself is cold and that it is only its movements which produce heat for; its effect is felt at so great a distance in space. The heat of the sun is the same as our natural fire; for as the sun is the centre of the planets and thence scatters its heat downward in all directions, so in the centre of the earth there is a sun of the earth, which by its perpetual motion drives heat or rays upward towards the surface of the earth. This inward heat is much more powerful than elemental fire but it is tempered and cooled by the water which pervades and refreshes the pores of the earth; otherwise all things would be consumed by its fierceness. In the same way, the fierce rays of the sun are tempered and assuaged by the air of the intermediate atmosphere, without which everything would be consumed, and no generation would be possible. But I must now proceed to explain after what manner the elements act upon each other. In the centre of the earth, then, there is a central sun, of which the heat pervades the whole earth to its surface by reason of the movement thereof, or by the motion of the firmament thereof. This heat changes the water of the earth into air (or vapour), which being much more subtle than water, is violently driven upward through the pores of the earth. But when it reaches the colder atmosphere it is once more condensed into water and in some places we do indeed see this water or condensed, air driven highly up into the air by the force of the central fire: just as a kettle of water when exposed to gentle heat sends upward a gentle stream of vapour and air, while the steam thickens and the upward movement becomes more intense when the fire is kindled into a blaze. By this action of the "central sun" the elements are distributed over the earth and each finds the place where it can grow. This upward current of air is not always noticeable because in many places there is not enough water to make it perceptible: an empty kettle gives out no steam I say, then, that fire or heat is the cause of the motion of the air, and the life of all things; and the earth is their nurse, or receptacle. If our earth and air were not cooled by water, the earth would be parched up, as it is even now in some places where the pores of the earth are closed up, and by obstructing the movement of the water would be placed at the mercy of the two kinds of solar heat. In this way the destruction of the world will one day be brought about. Now in our Art you should closely imitate these natural processes. There should be the Central Heat, the change of the water into air, the driving upward of the air, its diffusion through the pores of the earth, its reappearance as condensed but volatilized water. Then you must give our Ancient One gold and silver to swallow and consume, till he himself is burnt to death and his ashes are scattered into the water, which you must then subject to coction for a sufficient space of time. The result will be the Medicine which is a cure for leprosy.

But be careful not to take heat for cold, or cold for heat. Mix only things which are like each other, and separate contrary elements by means of heat. If you do not follow the guidance of Nature all your efforts will be in vain. I swear by God that I have spoken to you as a father should to his son. He that hath ears, let him hear, and he that hath sense, let him understand.

TWELFTH TREATISE

CONCERNING THE STONE AND ITS VIRTUE

We have spoken sufficiently in preceding chapters concerning the production of natural things, the elements, the first and second matters, bodies and seeds, as also of their use and virtue. I have written also of the Philosophical Stone, and shall now speak of its virtue, in so far as experience has discovered it to me. Before, however, I proceed to describe the virtues of the Stone, I will, for the better understanding of our Art, once more recapitulate what has already been said. If any one doubts the reality of our Art, he should read the books of those ancient Sages whose good faith no one ever yet called in question, and whose right to speak on this subject cannot be challenged. If you will not believe them, I am not so foolish as to enter into a controversy with one who denies first principles: the deaf and dumb cannot speak. Why minerals alone should be excluded from God's primal benediction, when He bade all things increase and multiply after their kind, I am unable to see; and if minerals have seed they have it for the purpose of generic propagation. The Art of Alchemy is true in its nature. Nature is true also, but a true Artist is rarely found. Nature is one, our Art is one but the workmen are many. Nature, then, generates things through the Will of God out of the first Matter (the product of the elements) which is known to God alone. Nature produces things, and multiplies them out of the second substance which is known to the Sages. All elements are mutually dependent, though they do not agree when joined, but the queen of all is water, because it is the mother of all things --and over it broods the spirit of fire. When fire acts on water, and strives with it, the first matter is evolved. Thus arise vapours of sufficient denseness to combine with earth, by means of that crude air which from the very beginning was separated from it. This process is going on ceaselessly, by means of perpetual motion. For motion causes heat, as you may know by continued friction of any substance. Motion causes heat, heat moves the water; the motion of water produces air, which is the life of all living things. Thus all things grow out of water, out of its more subtle vapours are produced light and subtle things; out of its "oil," things of greater weight; out of its salt things far more beautiful and precious than the rest. But as Nature is often hindered by the impurity of this vapour, fatness, and salt, from producing perfection, experience has taught us to separate the pure from the impure. Therefore, if you would ameliorate Nature, and produce a more perfect and elaborated subject, purge the body by dissolution of all that is heterogeneous, and unite the pure to the pure, the well-digested to the well-digested, and the crude to the crude, according to the natural and not the material weight. For you must know that the central saltpetre never contains more earth than is required whether it be otherwise pure or impure. But it is different with the fatness of the water, which is never found pure. Art purges it by the action of twofold heat, and then again combines its elements.

EPILOGUE

OR CONCLUSION OF THESE TWELVE TREATISES

I have composed, O friendly reader, the preceding twelve treatises for the benefit of the students of this Art; in order that they might understand the operations of Nature, and after what manner she produces all things which are in the world, before they put their hands to any experiment. Otherwise, they might be trying to open the gate without a key, or to draw water with a sieve. For in regard to our Holy and Blessed Art, he for whom the sun shines not, walks in thick darkness, and he who does not see the light of the moon, is involved in the shades of night. Nature has her own light, which is not visible to the outward eyes. The shadow of Nature upon our eyes is the body. But where the light of Nature irradiates the mind, this mist is cleared away from the eyes, all difficulties are overcome, and things are seen in their very essence, namely, the inmost heart of our Magnesia, which corresponds to the respective centres of the Sun and Earth. The bodily nature of things is a concealing outward vesture. If you dressed a boy and a girl of twelve years of age in exactly the same way, you would be puzzled to tell which was the boy and which the girl, but when the clothes are removed they may easily be distinguished. In the same way, our understanding makes a shadow to the shadow of Nature, for our human nature is concealed by the body in the same way as the body by the clothes. I might in this place discourse fully and philosophically of the dignity of man, of his creation and generation but I will pass over these themes and touch briefly on his life alone. Man is made of earth, and lives through air; for air contains the hidden food of life, of which the invisible spirit, when congealed is better than the whole world. Truly wonderful and admirable are the ways of Nature, who shews to us day by day the light of truth. I have set down in these twelve Treatises that which she has revealed to me in order that the God-fearing reader may more easily understand that which I have seen with my eyes, that which my hands have performed, without any fraud or sophistication. For without the light and knowledge of Nature it is impossible to attain to the perfection of this Art, unless it be revealed to a man by the Spirit, or secretly by a loving friend. The substance is vile and yet most precious. Take ten parts of our air; one part of living gold or living silver; put all this into your vessel; subject the air to coction until it becomes first water and then something which is not water. If you do not know how to do this and how to cook air, you will go wrong, for herein is the true Matter of the Philosophers. You must take that which is, but is not seen until the operator pleases. This is the water of our dew, which is extracted from the saltpetre of the Sages, by which all things grow, exist, and are nourished, whose womb is the centre of the celestial and terrestrial sun and moon. To speak more openly, it is our Magnet, which I have already called our Chalybs, or steel. Air generates this magnet, the magnet engenders or manifests our air. Thus Hermes says that its father is the Sun, its mother the Moon, and that the winds have fostered it in their womb, that is to say, the salt Alkali (called by the Sages salt of Ammonia, or vegetable salt) is hidden in the womb of Magnesia. The operation thereof is as follows: --- You dissolve condensed air, and in it a tenth part of gold; seal it up and expose it to our fire, until the air is changed into powder and there will be seen, given the salt of the world, a great variety of colours. The rest of this process and the method of multiplication you will find fully set forth in the writings of Lullius, and other of the ancient Sages, so therefore I do not dwell on them being content to treat only of the first and second matters. This I have done frankly, and with open heart. Think not that any man in this world has spoken more fully and clearly than I have. I have not learnt what I tell you from books, but by the experiment of my own hands. If you do not understand it at first, or are unable to accept the truth, accuse not my work, but blame rather yourself, believing that God will not reveal this secret unto you. Take it, then, in all earnestness, read and again read it, especially the Epilogue of these twelve Treatises, and diligently consider the possibilities of Nature, the action of the elements, and which is chief among them, especially in the rarefaction of air or water, by which the heavens and the whole world were created. This I admonish you to do, as a father admonishes a son. Do not wonder that I have written so many Treatises. I am not in need of books for myself but was impelled to record my experience by pity towards those who are wandering astray in the darkness of their own conceits; and though I might have set forth this secret in few words, I have written at great length in order to equip you with that knowledge of Nature, without which you could not hope to succeed in this Art. Do not be put out by the seeming contradictions with which, in accordance with the custom of the Sages, I have had to conceal my real meaning a little. There is no rose found without thorns. Revolve diligently in your mind all that I have said about the way in which the elements distil the Radical Moisture to the centre of the earth, and how the terrestrial and centric sun again raises and sublimes them, by its continual motion, to the surface of the earth. Note also the correspondence which has been affirmed between the celestial and the centric Sun for the celestial Sun and Moon have a special power and a wonderful virtue in distilling upon earth by their rays. For heat is easily united to heat, and salt to salt. As the central sun has its sea and crude perceptible water, so the celestial sun has its sea of subtle and imperceptible water (the atmosphere). On the surface of the earth the two kinds of rays meet and produce flowers and all things. Then rain receives its vital force out of the air, and unites it to that of the saltpetre of the earth. For the saltpetre of the earth is like calcined tartar, and by its dryness, attracts air to itself --- which air it dissolves into water. For this saltpetre itself was once air, and has become joined to the fatness of the earth. The more abundantly the rays of the sun descend, the greater is the quantity of saltpetre generated, and so also is the harvest on earth increased. All this does experience daily teach. I have willed thus to set forth solely for the benefit of the ignorant the correspondences which exist between all things, and the efficacious virtue of the Sun, Moon, and Stars. The wise have no need of such instruction. Our substance is openly displayed before the eyes of all, and yet is not known. Oh, how marvellous is our heaven, and our water, and our mercury, and our saltpetre which are in the world sea, and our vegetable, and our fixed and volatile sulphur, and our dead head, or dregs of our sea, and our water that does not wet the hands, and without which no mortal can live --- without which nothing is born or generated in the whole world! It is lightly esteemed by men, yet no one can do without it: for it is more precious than all the world beside, and, in short, it is nothing but our pontic-water which is congealed in the sun and moon and extracted from the sun and moon, by means of our chalybs (steel) through the skill of the Sages by a philosophical artifice and in a surprising manner... I did not really intend to publish this book, for reasons that are named in the preface; but my love for earnest students of this Art got the better of my caution. So have I sought to make known my good-will to those who knows me, and manifest unto the initiated that I am their companion and equal, and that I desire their acquaintance. I doubt not that there are many persons of good conduct and clear conscience who possess this great gift of God in secret. I pray and conjure them that they should preserve even the silence of Harpocrates. Let them be made wise by my example, and take warning from my dangers. Whenever I have revealed myself to the great, it has always been to my peril and loss. But by this work I now shew myself to the Sons of Hermes, while at the same time I instruct the ignorant, and direct lost seekers into the right path. Let them know that the secret is here as plainly expounded as it ever will be. I have kept nothing back except the secret of extracting our "salt of Ammonia," or " Mercury of the Sages " out of our "sea water," and the great use to which it is put. If I have not expressed myself very plainly on these points, it is only because I may not do so. The secret can only be revealed by God, who knows men's hearts and minds, and He will vouchsafe this knowledge, in answer to earnest and importunate prayer after a repeated careful perusal of this Book. The vessel, as I have said, is one, or two at most will suffice; and if you have knowledge of Nature, a continuous fire, and the right substance, you ought to succeed. Let me caution you, in conclusion, not to be led astray by those who waste their time and money on herbs, animals, stones, and all kinds of minerals but the right ones. Farewell, good reader, and may you long enjoy the results of my labours, to the glory of God, the salvation of your soul, and the good of your neighbour.

A PREFACE TO THE RIDDLE OF THE SAGES

ADDRESSED TO THE SONS OF TRUTH

Though I have already given unto you, O Children of Science, a full and exhaustive account of our Art, and of the source of the universal fountain, so that there seems no further call to say anything, having, in the preceding Treatises, illustrated the mode of Nature by examples, and declared both the theory and the practice, so far it is permitted me to do, yet there may be some of my readers who think that I have expressed myself here and there in too laconical a fashion. I will therefore once more make known from beginning to end the entire process, but in the form of a philosophical enigma, so that you may judge how far I have been permitted to attain by God. There is an infinite number of books which treat of this Art, but you will scarce find any which contain a more clear explication of the truth than is here set down. I have, in the course of my life, met with a good many who fancied that they had a perfect understanding of the writings of the Sages; but their subtle style of interpretation was in glaring contrast with the simplicity of Nature, and they laughed at what they were pleased to call the rustic crudeness of my remarks. I have also frequently attempted to explain our Art to others by word of mouth; but though they called themselves Sages, they would not believe that there is such water in our sea, and attributed my remarks to temporary insanity. For this reason I am not afraid that my writings will reveal anything to unworthy persons, as <u>I am persuaded that it is only by the gift of God that this Art can be understood</u>. If, indeed, subtlety and mental acuteness were all that is necessary for its apprehension, I have met with many strong minds, well fitted for the investigation of such subjects. But I tell you: Be simple, and not overwise, until you have found the secret. Then you will be obliged to be prudent, and you will easily be able to compose any number of books, which is doubtless more simple for him who is in the centre and beholds the thing itself, than one who is on the circumference only, and can only go by hearsay. You have a clear description of the matter of all things, but I warn you that if you would attain to this knowledge you should continue in earnest prayer to God, and love your neighbour. In the second place, you should not be ready to imagine all manner of subtleties and refinements of which Nature knows nothing. Remain rather in the way of her simplicity, for therein you are far more likely to put your finger on the subject than if you abide in the midst of subtleties.

In reading my book, do not stick too closely to the letter of my words but read them side by side with the natural facts which they describe. You should also from the first fix your eyes steadily on the object of your search, and the scope and aim of our work. It is much wiser to learn with your mind and your brain first than by bitter experience afterwards. The object of your search should be to find a hidden thing from which, by a marvellous artifice, there is obtained a liquid by whose means gold is dissolved as gently and naturally as ice is melted in warm water. If you can find this substance, you have that out of which Nature produced gold, and though all metals and all things are derived from it, yet it takes most kindly to gold. For all other things are clogged with impurity, except gold wherein there is no uncleanness, whence in a special manner this matter is, as it were, the mother of gold. If you will not follow my instructions, and be warned by my cautions, you can derive no benefit from my book. I have spoken as plainly as my conscience would permit. If you ask who I am: I am a Cosmopolitan. If you know me, and wish to be good and honourable men, keep my name a secret. If you do not know me forbear to enquire after my name, for I shall make public nothing more than appears in this writing. Believe me, if my rank and station were not what they are, I should enjoy nothing so much as a solitary life, or to have joined Diogenes in his tub. For I behold this world full of vanity, greed, cruelty, venality, and iniquity; and I rejoice in the prospect of the glorious life to come. I no longer wonder, as once I did, that the true Sage, though he owns the Stone, does not care to prolong his life; for he daily sees heaven before his eyes, as you see your face in a glass. When God gives you what you desire, you will believe me, and not make yourself known to the world.

A PARABLE, OR ENIGMA OF THE SAGES

ADDED BY WAY OF AN APPENDIX

Once upon a time, when I had been for many years of my life sailing from the Arctic to he Antarctic Pole, I was cast ashore by the will of God, on the coast of a certain great ocean; and though I was well acquainted with the properties of that sea, I did not know whether there was generated near those shores that little fish Edieneis, which is so anxiously sought, even unto this present, by men of high and low degree. But as I watched the Naiads and Nymphs disporting themselves in the water, being fatigued with my previous toils, and overwhelmed by the multitude of my thoughts, I was lulled asleep by the soft murmur of the waves; and as I slept sweetly and gently, I beheld a marvellous vision I saw ancient Neptune, with a trident in his hand, rise, with venerable aspect, from our sea, who after a friendly salutation, carried me to a most beautiful island. This island was situated in the southern hemisphere, and contained all that is required for man's use and delight. It appeared a more pleasant and delightful abode than Virgil's Elysian fields. The shores thereof were fringed with verdant myrtles and cypresses.

The meadows were studded with a large variety of beautiful and fragrant flowers. The slopes of the hills were clad with vines, olives, and cedars. The roads were overhung by the intertwining branches of laurels and pomegranate trees, which afforded grateful shade to the wayfarer. The plains were covered with groves of orange and lemon trees. In short, the island was an epitome of earthly beauty. Concealed under a rock, Neptune shewed me two minerals of that island, gold and chalybs (steel). Then I was conducted to an orchard in the middle of a meadow, which was at no great distance, the same being planted with a great variety of beautiful trees. Among these he shewed me seven enriched by particular names; and two of them towered above the rest. One bore fruit which shone like the sun, and its leaves resembled gold; the fruit of the other was whiter than lilies, and its leaves were like fine silver. <u>Neptune called the first the Solar, and the second he Lunar tree.</u> The only thing which it was difficult to obtain in the island, was water. The inhabitants had tried to get it from a spring by means of a conduit, and to elicit it from many things But the result was a poisonous water, and the only water that could be drunk was that condensed out of the rays of the sun and moon. The worst of it was, that no one could attract more than ten parts of this water. It was wonderful water! I can tell vou; for I saw with my eyes and touched with my hands its dazzling whiteness, which surpassed all the splendour of the now. While I stood wrapt in admiration, Neptune vanished from my sight, and there stood before me a tall man, on whose forehead the name of Saturn was inscribed. He took a vessel, and scooped up ten parts of the water, in which he placed fruit from the Solar tree; and the fruit was consumed like ice in warm water. So I said unto him: "Lord, I behold here a marvellous thing. This water is small in quantity; nevertheless, the fruit of this tree is consumed therein by a gentle heat. To what purpose is all this? "He graciously replied " My son, it is true that this thing is wonderful. But this water is the water of life, and has such power to exalt the qualities of this fruit, that it shall afterwards, without sowing or planting -- only by its fragrance -- transmute the six trees which remain into its own nature. Moreover, this water is as a woman to the fruit: the fruits of this tree can putrefy nowhere but in this water; and though the fruit by itself be wonderful and precious -- yet when it putrefies in this water, it brings forth out of this putrefaction a Salamander that endures the fire; its blood is more precious than all treasures, and has power to render fertile trees such as you see here, and to make their fruit sweeter than honey" Then I said unto him: "Lord, how is this thing done?" He replied: "I have already told thee that the fruits of the Solar tree are living, and they are sweet; but whereas the fruit while it is cooked in this water can inform but one part, after its coction has been completed it can inform a thousand." I then enquired whether the fruit was boiled in this water over a fierce fire, and how long? He answered this water has an inward fire, and when this is assisted by continuous outward warmth, it burns up three parts of its own body with this body of the fruit, until nothing but an incredibly small part remains, which, however, possesses the most marvellous virtue. This is cooked by the wise Master first for seven months, and then for ten. But in the meantime, on each fiftieth day, a variety of phenomena is witnessed." Again I besought him whether this fruit was cooked in several waters and whether anything was added to it. He made answer: "There is no water, either in this island or in the whole country but only this kind alone that can properly penetrate the pores of this fruit; and you should know the Solar tree also grew out of this water, which is collected by magnetic attraction out of the rays of the Sun and Moon. Hence the fruit and the water exhibit a wonderful sympathy and correspondence. If any foreign substance were added to the water, its virtue would only be impaired. Hence nothing should be put into the water but this fruit. After its decoction the fruit has life and blood, and its blood causes all barren trees to bring forth the same precious fruit." I asked whether the water was obtained by any secret process, or whether it was to be obtained everywhere? He said: "It is found everywhere, and no one can live without it, but it is best when extracted by means of our Chalybs (steel), as which is found in the belly of the Ram. If you ask what is its use, I answer that before the due amount of coction has been performed, it is deadly poison, but afterwards it is the Great Medicine, and yields 29 grains of blood, each one of which produces 864 of the fruits of the Solar tree." I asked whether it could be still further improved. "The Sages say," he returned, "that it can be increased first to ten, then to a hundred, then to a thousand, then to ten thousand times its own quantity, and so on." I asked whether that water was known by any particular name. He cried aloud saying: "Few know it, but all have seen it, and see and love it; it has many names, but we call it the water of our sea the water that does not wet the hands." "Do they use it for any other purpose?" I enquired; "and is anything born in it?" "Every created thing," he replied, "uses it, but invisibly. All things owe their birth to it, and live in it. Nothing is, properly speaking, in it, though itself mingles with all things. It can be improved by nothing but the fruit of the Solar trees without which it is of no use in this work." I was going to ask him to speak more plainly when he began to cry out in such a loud voice that I awoke out of my sleep, and Saturn and the hope of getting my questions answered vanished together. Be contented, nevertheless, with what I have told you, and be sure that it is impossible to speak more clearly. If you do not understand what I have said, you will never grasp the writing of other philosophers. After a while, I fell into another deep sleep, in which I saw Neptune standing over me, congratulating me on our happy meeting in the Garden of the Hesperides. He held up to me a mirror, in which I saw the whole of Nature unveiled. After we had exchanged a few remarks, I thanked him for conducting me to this beautiful garden, and introducing me to the company of Saturn; and I heartily besought him to resolve for me the difficulties and doubts which Saturn had left uncleared. "For instance," I said, " I have read and believe that for every act of generation a male and a female are required; and yet Saturn spoke of generation by placing the Solar fruit in the water, or Mercury of the Sages. What did he mean? As the lord of the sea, I know that you are acquainted with these things, and I entreat of you to answer me." He said, "What you say about the act of generation is true; and yet you know that worms are produced in a different way from quadrupeds, namely by putrefaction and the place or earth in which this putrefaction occurs is feminine. In our substance the Mother is the water of which so much has been said, and its offspring is produced by putrefaction, after the manner of worms. Hence the Sages call it the Phoenix and Salamander. Its generation is a resurrection rather than a birth, and for this reason it is immortal or indestructible. Now, whatsoever is conceived of two bodies is subject to the law of death; but the life of this fruit is a separation from all that is corruptible about it. It is the same with the Phoenix, which separates of itself from its corruptible body." I enquired whether the substance was compound in its nature. "No," he said, "there is only the Solar fruit that is put into the water which must be to the fruit in the proportion of ten to one. Believe that what was here revealed to you in a dream by Saturn after the manner of our island, is not a dream, but a bright reality which will stand the test of broad daylight." With these words he abruptly left me, without listening to my further questions; and I awoke and found myself at home in

Europe. My God shew to you, gentle reader, the full interpretation of my dreams! Farewell!

TO THE TRIUNE GOD BE PRAISE AND GLORY!

A DIALOGUE BETWEEN MERCURY, THE ALCHEMISTS, AND NATURE

On a certain bright morning a number of Alchemists met together in a meadow, and consulted as to the best way of preparing the Philosopher's Stone. It was arranged that they should speak in order, and each after the manner that seemed best to him. <u>Most of them agreed that Mercury was the first substance</u>. Others said, no, it was sulphur, or something else. These Alchemists had read the books of the Sages, and hence there was a decided majority in favour of Mercury, not only as the true first matter, but in particular as the first matter of metals, since all the philosophers seemed to cry with one voice: "O our Mercury, our Mercury," &c., whatever that word might mean. Just as the dispute began to run high, there arose a violent wind which dispersed the Alchemists into all the different countries of the world -- and as they had arrived at no conclusion, each one went on seeking the Philosopher's Stone in his own old way, this one expecting to find it in one substance, and that in another, so that the search has continued without intermission even unto this day. One of them, however, had at least got the idea into his head that Mercury was the substance of the Stone, and determined to concentrate all his efforts on the chemical preparation of Mercury saying to himself, for this kind of discourse is very common among Alchemists, that the assembly had determined nothing, and that the dispute would end only with the confection of the Stone. So he began reading the works of the philosophers, and among others that of Alanus on Mercury, whereby he became a philosopher indeed, but not one who had reached any practical conclusion. Then he took (common) Mercury and began to work with it. He placed it in a glass vessel over the fire, where it, of course, evaporated. So in his ignorance he struck his wife and said "No one but you has entered my laboratory; you must have taken my Mercury out of the vessel." The woman, with tears, protested her innocence. The Alchemist put some more Mercury into the vessel, and kept close and jealous watch over it, expecting that his wife would once more make away with it. The Mercury rose to the top of the vessel in vaporous steam. Then the Alchemist was full of joy, because he remembered that the first substance of the Stone is described by the Sages as volatile; and he thought that now at last he must be on the right track. He now began to subject the Mercury to all sorts of chemical processes, to sublime it, and to calcine it with all manner of things, with salts, sulphur, metals, minerals, blood, hair, aqua fortis, herbs, urine, and vinegar. All these substances were tried in succession, everything that he could think of was tried; but without producing the desired effect. Seeing that he had still accomplished nothing, the poor man once more began to take thought with himself. At last he remembered reading in some authors that the matter was so contemptible that it is found on the dung hill; and then he began to operate on his Mercury with various kinds of dung. When all these experiments turned out failures, he fell into a deep sleep, and there appeared to him an old man, who elicited from him the cause of his sadness, and bade him use the pure Mercury of the Sages. When the Alchemist awoke he pondered over the words of the old man, and wondered what he could mean by "the Mercury of the Sages". But he could think of no other Mercury but that known to the common herd, and went on with his efforts to purge it; for which purpose he used, first, the excrements of animals, then those of children, and at last his own. He also went every day to the place where the old man had appeared to him, in the hope that he might be able to ask him for a more detailed explanation of his meaning. At times, he would pretend to be asleep; and because he thought that the old man might be afraid to come to him in his waking hours, he would swear to him, and say: "Be not afraid to come, old man I am most certainly asleep. See, my eyes are tightly shut". At length, from always thinking about that old man, he fell into a fever, and in his delirious visions he at last saw a phantom in the guise of that ancient standing at his bedside, and heard him say "Do not despair, my friend. Your mercury is good, and your substance is good, but it will not obey you. Why do you not charm the mercury, as serpents are charmed? " With this, the old man vanished. But the Alchemist arose, with these words still ringing in his ears: "Serpents are charmed" -- and recollecting that apothecaries ornament their mercury bottles with images of serpents, he took up the vessel with the mercury, and repeated the formula of conjuration "ux, ux, ostas," etc., substituting the word mercury for the name of the serpent: "And thou mercury, most nefarious beast." At these words the Mercury began to laugh, and said to the Alchemist "Why dost thou trouble me, my Lord Alchemist?"

ALCHEMIST: Oho, do you call me your lord? Now I have touched you home. I have found a bit to bridle you with; wait a little, and you shall soon sing the tune that I bid you (Then as his courage increased, he cried angrily): I conjure you by the living God -- are you not that Mercury of the Sages?

MERCURY: (pretending to speak in a whimpering and frightened tone of voice): Master, I am Mercury.

ALCHEMIST: Why would you not obey me then? Why could I not fix you?

MERCURY: Oh, most high and mighty Master, I implore you to spare your miserable slave! I did not know that you were such a potent philosopher.

ALCHEMIST: Oh, could you not guess as much from the philosophical way in which I operated on you?

MERCURY: I did so, most high and mighty Master, but I wished to hide myself, though now I see that I cannot hide myself from my most potent Lord.

ALCHEMIST: Then you know a philosopher when you see him, as you now do, my gallant?

MERCURY: My most high Lord, I see, and to my own great cost, that your Worship is a high and mighty and most potent philosopher.

ALCHEMIST: (with a smile of satisfaction): Now at last I have found what I sought (To the Mercury, in awful tones of thunder): Now mind that you obey me, else it will be the worse for you.

MERCURY: Gladly, Master, if I can for I am very weak.

ALCHEMIST: Oho, do you begin to make excuses already?

MERCURY: No, but I am very languid.

ALCHEMIST: What is the matter with you?

MERCURY: An Alchemist is the matter with me.

ALCHEMIST: Are you laughing at me, you false rogue?

MERCURY: Oh, no, no, Master, as God shall spare me, I spoke of an Alchemist - you are a philosopher.

ALCHEMIST: Of course, of course, that is quite true. But what did the Alchemist do?

MERCURY: Oh Master, he has done me a thousand wrongs; he beloboured and mixed me up with all manner of disagreeable and contradictory things, which have stripped me of all my powers and so I am sick, even to death.

ALCHEMIST: You deserved such treatment, because you would not obey.

MERCURY: I never yet disobeyed a philosopher, but I cannot help laughing at fools.

ALCHEMIST: And what is your opinion of me?

MERCURY: Oh, Master your Worship is a great man, and mighty philosopher, greater by far than Hermes, both in doctrine and wisdom.

ALCHEMIST: Well, I won't praise myself, but I certainly am a learned man. My wife says so, too. She always calls me a profoundly learned philosopher.

MERCURY: I quite believe you. For philosophers are men whom too much learning and thought have made mad.

ALCHEMIST: Tell me, what am I to do with you? How am I to make you into the Philosopher's Stone?

MERCURY: Oh, my master philosopher, that I cannot tell. You are a philosopher, I am the philosopher's humble slave. Whatever he wishes to make me, I become, as far as my nature will allow.

ALCHEMIST: This is all very fine, but I repeat that you must tell me how to treat you, and whether you can become the Philosopher's Stone.

MERCURY: Mr. Philosopher, if you know, you can make it, and if you don't you can't. From me you cannot learn anything with which you have been unacquainted beforehand.

ALCHEMIST: You talk to me as to a simple person. Perhaps you do not know that I have lived at the courts of great princes, and have always been regarded as a very profound philosopher.

MERCURY: I readily believe you, my Master for the filth of your brilliant experiments still cleaves to me.

ALCHEMIST: Tell me then, are you the Mercury of the Sages?

MERCURY: I am Mercury, but you should know best, whether I am the Mercury of you philosophers.

ALCHEMIST: Tell me only whether you are the true Mercury or whether there is another?

MERCURY: I am Mercury, but there is also another.

With these words the Mercury vanished. The Alchemist shouts and calls aloud, but there is no answer. At last he is fain to derive some little comfort from the thought that he has had speech of Mercury and therefore must be very dear to it. With this thought he once more sets himself to sublime, distil, calcine, precipitate, and dissolve the Mercury in the most awful manner, and with different sorts of waters. But his efforts turned out failures, and mere waste of time. Then he began to curse Mercury and to blaspheme Nature for creating it. When nature heard this, she called Mercury to her, and asked him what he had done to the Alchemist, and why he would not obey him. Mercury humbly protested his innocence. Nature admonished him to obey the Sons of Knowledge who sought to know her. Mercury promised that he would do so, but added: "Mother Nature who can satisfy fools?" Nature smiled, and departed. Mercury indignant with our Alchemist, returned also to his own place. The philosopher presently appeared with some excrements of swine, and was proceeding to ply Mercury therewith, when the latter thus wrathfully accosted him: "What do you want of me, you fool? Why did you accuse me?"

ALCHEMIST: Are you he whom I so much desire to see?

MERCURY: I am; but blind people cannot behold me.

ALCHEMIST: I am not blind.

MERCURY: You are as blind as a new-born puppy. You cannot see yourself: how then should you be able to see me?

ALCHEMIST: Oh, now you are proud and despise me because I speak humbly. Perhaps you do not know that I have lived at the courts of princes, and have always been called a philosopher?

MERCURY: The gates of princes stand wide for fools; and it is they that fare sumptuously in the palaces of the great. I quite believe that you have been at court.

ALCHEMIST: You are, undoubtedly, the Devil, and not a good Mercury, if you speak like that to philosophers.

MERCURY: Now, in confidence, tell me whether you are acquainted with any philosophers.

ALCHEMIST: Do you ask this of me, when you are aware that I am myself a philosopher?

MERCURY: (smiling): Behold the Philosopher! Well, my philosopher, what do you seek, and what would you have?

ALCHEMIST: The Philosopher's Stone.

MERCURY: Of what substance would you make it?

ALCHEMIST: Of our Mercury.

MERCURY: Oh, my philosopher, then I had better go: for I am not yours!

ALCHEMIST: You are none but the Devil, and wish to lead me astray.

MERCURY: Well, my philosopher, I think I may return the compliment: you have played the very devil with me.

ALCHEMIST: Oh, what do I hear? This is most certainly the Devil. For I have done everything most scientifically, according to the writings of the Sages.

MERCURY: Truly, you are a wonderful operator; your performances exceed your knowledge by as much as they defy the authorities which you have in your books. For they say that substances should be mixed only with substances of a kindred nature. But you have mixed me, against Nature, with dung and other foul things, and are indifferent about defiling yourself so long as you can torture me.

ALCHEMIST: I do nothing against Nature: I only sow the seed in its own proper earth, according to the teaching of the Sages.

MERCURY: You sow me in dung; at the time of the harvest I vanish, and you reap dung. Verily, you are a good husbandman!

ALCHEMIST: Yet the Sages say that their substance is found on the dunghill.

MERCURY: What they say is true, but you understand only the letter, and not the spirit of their injunctions.

ALCHEMIST: Now I see that you are perhaps Mercury. But as you will not obey me, I must once more repeat the words of conjuration: Ux, ux, ostas ----

MERCURY: (laughing): It is of no use, my friend; your words are as profitable as your works.

ALCHEMIST: They say true when they call you a wonderful and inconstant and volatile substance.

MERCURY: You call me inconstant. But to the constant I am also constant, and to the man of fixed resolve, I am fixed. But you, and the likes of you, are continually abandoning one substance for another, and are ever vagabonds in experiment.

ALCHEMIST: Tell me truly, are you the Mercury which, side by side with sulphur and salt, the philosophers describe as the first principle of all things, or must I look for some other substance?

MERCURY: The fruit, when it falls, lies near the tree that bore it. I am the same that I was except in the matter of age. In the beginning I was young, and I remained so as long as I was alone. Now, I am old, and yet I am the same as ever. I am only older than I was.

ALCHEMIST: I am glad that you are old. For it is a constant and fixed substance that I require, and this also have I invariably sought.

MERCURY: It is in vain that you come to the old man whom you did not know as a youth.

ALCHEMIST: What is this you say ? Did I not know you when you were young? Have I not subjected you to all manner of chemical processes, and shall I not continue to do so till I have prepared the Philosopher's Stone?

MERCURY: Woe is me! What shall I do? I already scent the foul odour of dung. Woe is me! I beseech you Master Philosopher, not to ply me with excrements of swine -- the foul smell will drive me hence. And what more do you want of me? Am I not obedient ? Do I not mingle with all things that you ask me to amalgamate with? Do I not suffer myself to be sublimated, precipitated, amalgamated, calcined? What more can I do ? I have submitted to be scourged and spat upon till my miserable plight might move a heart of stone. I have given you milk, blood, flesh, butter, oil, and water. I have done all that any metal or mineral can do. And yet you have no pity on me! Woe is me !

ALCHEMIST: Oho, it does you no harm, you rascal, you deserve it all richly, for not changing your form, or for resuming the old form after a mere temporary change!

MERCURY: I do whatsoever you make me do. If you make me a body, I am a body. If you make me powder, I am powder. How can I be more obedient than I am ?

ALCHEMIST: Tell me, then, what you are in your centre, and I will not torment you any more.

MERCURY: I see there is no escape from speaking fundamentally to you. If you will, you may now understand me. With my form which you see you have nothing to do. My centre is the fixed heart of all things, immortal and all-pervading. I am a faithful servant to my master, and a faithful friend to my companions, whom I do not desert, and with whom I perish. I am an immortal body. I die when I am slain, but rise to stand before the judgment seat of a discriminating judge.

ALCHEMIST: Are you then the Philosopher's Stone?

MERCURY: My mother is such, and of her is born artificially some one thing -- but my brother who lives in the citadel has in his gift that which the Sage desires.

ALCHEMIST: Tell me, is your age great ?

MERCURY: My mother bore me yet I am older than my mother.

ALCHEMIST: How in all the world am I to understand you if you answer my questions in dark parables? Tell me in one word, are you that fountain concerning which Bernard Count of Trevisan, has written?

MERCURY: I am no fountain but I am water, and the fountain surrounds me.

ALCHEMIST: Since-you are water, is gold dissolved in you?

MERCURY: Whatever is with me, I love; and to that which is born with me I impart nourishment. That which is naked I cover with my wings.

ALCHEMIST: I see plainly that it is impossible to talk to you. Whatever I ask you, your reply is foreign to the point. If you do not answer my questions better, I will torment you again.

MERCURY: Have pity on me. Master, I will gladly tell you all I know.

ALCHEMIST: Tell me are you afraid of the fire?

MERCURY: I myself am fire.

ALCHEMIST: Why then do you seek to escape from the fire?

MERCURY: Because my spirit loves the spirit of the fire, and accompanies it wherever it goes.

ALCHEMIST: Where do you go when you ascend with the fire?

MERCURY: Every pilgrim looks anxiously towards his country and his home. When he has returned unto these he reposes, and he always comes back wiser than he left.

ALCHEMIST: Do you return, then?

MERCURY: Yes, but in another form.

ALCHEMIST: I do not understand what you mean, nor yet about the fire.

MERCURY: If any one knows the fire of my heart; he has seen that fire (proper heat) is my food; and the longer the spirit of my heart feeds on fire, the fatter will it be: its death is afterwards the life of all things belonging to my kingdom.

ALCHEMIST: Are you great?

MERCURY: My body, as you must know, can become one drop out of a thousand drops, and, though I am always one, you can divide my body as often as you like. But my spirit, or heart, always produces many thousands of parts out of one part.

ALCHEMIST: How is this to be brought about? After what manner should my operation be performed on you?

MERCURY: I am fire within, fire is my food and my life; but the life of fire is air, for without air fire is extinguished. Fire is stronger than air; hence I know not any repose, and crude air can neither coagulate nor restrain me. Add air to air, so that both become one in even balance; combine them with fire, and leave the whole to time.

ALCHEMIST: What will happen then?

MERCURY: Everything superfluous will be removed. The residue you burn in fire, place in water "cook," and when it is cooked you give as a medicine, and have no fear.

ALCHEMIST: You do not answer my questions. Wife, bring the excrements of swine, and we will see whether we can get the better of his stubbornness. In his utmost extremity, Mercury called in the help of Nature, amidst much lamentation and mourning over these threats of our admirable Alchemist. He impeaches the thankless operator; Nature trusts her son Mercury, whom she knows to be true and faithful and comes full of wrath to the Alchemist, calling him imperiously before her.

ALCHEMIST: Who calls me?

NATURE: What are you doing to my son, arch-fool that you are? Why do you torment him? He is willing to give you every blessing, if you can understand him.

ALCHEMIST: Who dares to rebuke so great a philosopher, and a man withal so excellent as I am?

NATURE: O fool, and of all men most insensate, I know and love all philosophers, and am loved of them. I take pleasure in aiding their efforts, and they help me to do that which I am unable to accomplish. But you so-called Alchemists are constantly offending me, and systematically doing despite to me; and this is the reason why all your efforts are doomed to failure.

ALCHEMIST: It is not true. I, too, am a philosopher, and understand scientific methods of procedure. I have lived with several princes, and with more than one philosopher, as my wife can testify. Moreover, I possess at this very moment a manuscript which has lain hidden for some centuries in a certain wall. I know very well that I am almost at the end of my labours, and am on the point of composing the Philosopher's Stone; for it was revealed to me a few days ago in a dream. I have had a great many dreams, nor do I ever dream anything untrue; my wife knows it.

NATURE: It is with you as with a great many of your fellows: at first they know everything, but in the end their knowledge turns to ignorance.

ALCHEMIST: If you are truly Nature, it is you who serve for the operation of the work.

NATURE: That is true; but it is performed only by those who know me, and such do not torment my children, nor do they hinder my working. Rather they clear away the impediments, that I may the sooner reach the goal.

ALCHEMIST: That is exactly what I do.

NATURE: No; you do nothing but cross me, and deal with my children against my will. Where you should revive you kill; where you should fix, you sublime; where you should calcine, you distil; and thus my obedient son Mercury you torment in the most fearful manner.

ALCHEMIST: Then I will in future deal with him gently, and subject him only to gradual coction.

NATURE: That is well, if you possess understanding; otherwise, you will ruin only yourself and your possessions. If you act in opposition to my commands, you hurt yourself more than him.

ALCHEMIST: But how am I to make the Philosopher's Stone?

NATURE: That question does not justify your ill treatment of my son. Know that I have many sons and daughters, and that I am swift to succour those who seek me, provided they are worthy.

ALCHEMIST: But who is that Mercury?

NATURE: Know that I have only one such son, he is one of seven, and the first among them; and though he is now all things, he was at first only one. In him are the four elements, yet he is not an element. He is a spirit, yet he has a body; a man, yet he performs a woman's part: a boy, yet he bears a man's weapons; a beast, and yet he has the wings of a bird. He is poison, yet he cures leprosy; life, yet he kills all things, a King, but another occupies his throne; he flees from the fire, yet fire is taken from him; he is water, but does not wet the hands; he is earth, and yet he is sown; he is air, and lives by water.

ALCHEMIST: Now I see that I know nothing; only I must not say so. For I should lose the good opinion of my neighbours, and they would no longer entrust me with money for my experiments. I must therefore go on saying that I know everything; for there are many that expect me to do great things for them.

NATURE: But if you go on in that way, your neighbours will at last find you out, and demand their money back.

ALCHEMIST: I must amuse them with promises, as long as I can.

NATURE: And what then?

ALCHEMIST: I will try different experiments; and if they fail, I will go to some other country, and live the same life there.

NATURE: And then?

ALCHEMIST: Ha, ha, ha ! There are many countries, and many greedy persons who will suffer themselves to be gulled by my promises of mountains of gold. Thus day will follow day, and in the meantime the King or the donkey will die, or I myself. Nature: Such philosophers are only fit for the gallows. Be off, and take with you my most grievous curse. The best thing that you can do, is to give yourself up to the King's officers, who will quickly put an end to you and your philosophy!

SECOND PART

CONCERNING SULPHUR

PREFACE

As I am not at liberty to write more plainly than the Ancient Sages, gentle Reader, you may possibly be dissatisfied with my Book, particularly as you have so many other philosophical treatises ready to your hand. But you may be sure that no necessity is laid upon me to write at all, and that if I have come forward it is only out of love to you, having no expectation of personal profit, and no desire for empty glory, for which reason I here refrain, as I have before done, from revealing my identity to the public. I was under the impression that in the first part of this work I had already given a lucid account of our whole Art. But my friends tell me that there is one point with which I have not yet fully dealt, and vehemently urge me to write this second treatise about Sulphur. The question is, whether even this Book will convey any information to one before whom the writings of the Sages and the Open Book of Nature are exhibited in vain. For if you could incline your ear to the teaching of Nature you would at once be able to emancipate yourself from the tutelage of printed volumes; in my opinion it is better to learn from the master himself than from one of the disciples.

In the preface to my twelve Treatises, and again in the twelfth chapter, I have already hinted at the reason why there is now so great a multitude of books on this subject, that they confound and hinder the student instead of helping him. The confusion is rendered worse confounded by the ill-will of the Sages, who seem to have set pen to paper for the express purpose of concealing their meaning; and by the carelessness with which some of the more important volumes are copied and printed; the sense of a whole passage is often hopelessly obscured by the addition or omission of one little word (e.g., the addition of the word "not" in the wrong place). Yet the student may get information even from these books (as the bee obtains honey even from poisonous flowers), if he reads them by the light of natural fact, and with constant reference to the utterances of other Sages. One writer explains another. Yet some of them are so closely beset with the difficulties of an obscure phraseology, that it is almost impossible to understand them, except by reading them side by side with the facts of Nature; for their interpreters and commentators are more hopelessly unintelligible even than the writers whom they take upon themselves to explain; the exposition is more difficult than the text. If you would succeed in this study, keep your eyes fixed on the possibilities of Nature, and on the properties of the natural substance. It is universally described as common and easy of access and apprehension, and it is so, but only to those who know it. He who knows it can discover it in the dunghill; he who does not will fail to find it even in gold I have no desire to praise myself, but this one thing I will say, that the reading of my Books, in combination with a careful study of Nature, and of the writings of other genuine possessors of this Stone, must in the end open up to you the understanding of this secret. If I have planted another tree in the dense forest of Alchemistic literature, I have done so, not in order to obstruct the path of students, but in order to aid and refresh them by the way. Let not the diligent and God-fearing enquirer despair. If he seek the inspiration of God he will most surely find it. This knowledge is more easily obtained of God than of men. For His mercy is infinite, and He never forsakes those who put their trust in Him; with Him there is no respect of persons, nor does He despise the humble and contrite heart. He has showered the fulness of His mercy even on me, the unworthiest of all His creatures, in shewing to me His wonderful power and ineffable goodness, which I am utterly unable to declare. The only way in which I can, in a small degree, at least prove my gratitude, is by succouring my struggling brother students with friendly counsel and assistance. Rest assured, then, gentle Reader, that He will grant this boon to you, if you wait upon Him day by day with earnest prayer, and in the power of a holy and loving life. He will throw open to you the portals of Nature; and you will be amazed at the simplicity of her operations. Know for certain that Nature is wonderfully simple; and that the characteristic mark of a childlike simplicity is stamped upon all that is true and noble in Nature. If you would imitate Nature, you should take her simplicity for your model in all the operations of Art. If my Book does not please you, throw it away, and take up some other author; it is short, so that you need not spend much time in reading it through. Only persevere: to the importunate knocker the door will at length be opened. The times are at hand when many secrets of Nature will be revealed to men. The Fourth or Northern Monarchy is about to be established; the Mother of Knowledge will soon come; and many things will be brought to light that were hidden under the three preceding monarchies. This fourth kingdom God will found by the hand of a prince who will be enriched with all virtues, and endowed with wisdom greater than that of Solomon. In his time (to adopt the words of the Psalmist) mercy and truth will meet together; peace and justice will kiss each other; truth will spring up from the ground, and righteousness will look down from heaven. There will be one Shepherd and one fold; and knowledge will be the common property of all. For those days I, too, am waiting with longing. Pray to God that it may come soon, gentle Reader. Fear Him, love Him, and- read carefully the books of His chosen Sages-and you will soon see, and behold with your own eyes, that I have spoken truly.

CONCERNING SULPHUR

The Second Principle SULPHUR is by no means the least important of the great principles, since it is a part of the metals and even a principal part of the Philosopher's Stone. Many Sages have left us weighty sayings about this substance: for instance, Geber himself ("Sum of Perfection," bk. I, chap. 28), who says: " It illumines all bodies, since it is the light of the light, and their tincture." But seeing that the ancients regarded it as the noblest principle, before we proceed to speak about it, we must first explain the origin of the three principles. The origin of the principles is a subject which has hitherto been but scantily discussed in the works of the Sages; and the student who knows nothing about it, is as much in the dark in regard to this matter, as is a blind man in respect to colour. I therefore propose to make this point which my predecessors have neglected, the subject of my treatise.

Now, according to the ancient Sages there are two principles of things, and more particularly of metals, namely, Sulphur and Mercury; according to the Moderns there are three: Salt, Sulphur, and Mercury, and the source of these principles are the elements; of which it therefore behoves us to speak first. Be it known to the students of this art that there are four elements, and that each has at its centre another element which makes it what it is. These are the four pillars of the world. They were in the beginning evolved and moulded out of chaos by the hand of the Creator; and it is their contrary action which keeps up the harmony and equilibrium of the mundane machinery; it is they which, through the virtue of celestial influences, produce all things above and beneath the earth. We will say a few words about each of them in due order of succession: and first of all about the nearest element, Earth.

CONCERNING ELEMENTARY EARTH

Earth is an element of considerable quality and dignity. In this element the other three, especially fire, are latent. It is admirably adapted both to the concealment and to the manifestation of things committed to it. It is gross and porous. specifically heavy, but naturally light. It is also the Centre of the World and of the other elements; through its centre passes the axis of the earth to both poles. It is porous, as we have said, like a sponge, and produces nothing of itself; but it receives all that the other three project into it, conscientiously conceals what it should hide, and brings to light that which it should manifest. Whatsoever is committed to it putrefies in it through the action of motive heat, and is multiplied by the separation of the pure from the impure. Heavy substances are hidden in it. Light substances are driven by heat to its surface. It is the nurse and womb of all seed and commixtion; and these seeds and compounds it faithfully preserves and fosters till the season of maturity. It is cold and dry, but its dryness is tempered with water; outwardly it is visible and fixed; inwardly it is invisible and volatile. It is a virgin substance, and dead residue of the creative distillation of the world, which

God will one day calcine, and after extracting the humour, create out of it a new crystalline earth. In its present state it consists of a pure and an impure element. The first is used by water for producing natural forms; the latter remains where it is. It is also the storehouse of all treasures, and in its centre is the Gehennal fire, conserving the machine of the world, and this by the expression of water, which it converts into air. This fire is produced by perpetual motion, and the influences of the Stars; it is aided by the Solar heat, which is tempered by the atmosphere, and the two together mature the growth of all things. For this reason the element of earth has fire intrinsically, and the earth is purified by this inward fire, as every element is purified by that which is in it. The inmost part, or centre of the earth, is then the highest purity mixed with fire, in which there is ceaseless motion, and we have shewn at some length in the twelve Treatises that it is, as it were, an empty space, into which the other elements project their products. It is enough for us to remember that this elementary earth is like a sponge, and the receptacle of all other elements.

CONCERNING ELEMENTARY WATER

Water is an element of great specific gravity, full of unctuous moisture. Outwardly it is volatile inwardly it is fixed, cold, and humid It is tempered by air, and is the sperm of the world, in which the seed of all things is conserved. There is a great difference between sperm and seed. Earth is the receptacle of sperm, water the receptacle of seed. Whatever the air, under the influence of fire, distils into the water, is imparted by the water to the earth. There is always an abundance of sperm awaiting seed, in order that it may carry it into the matrix, which is performed by the movement of the air, excited by the imagination of fire. Sometimes sperm has not a sufficient quantity of seed, for want of heat to digest it Sometimes, when there is no seed, the sperm enters the womb alone, but is ejected again without producing any fruit. At other times conception does not take place, even when there is plenty of seed in the sperm, because the womb is rendered barren by a superfluity of bad sulphur and malignant phlegm. Water is capable of commixtion with all things, by means of its volatile surface; it purifies and dissolves earth; air is congealed in it, and thus intimately united to it. It is the Solvent of the

85

World, because by the action of heat, it penetrates the air, and carries with it a warm vapour which causes the natural generation of those things with which the earth is like a womb impregnated. When the womb has once received a due portion of seed, Nature never rests until the natural form (whatever it may be) has been produced. The humid residue, or sperm, is putrefied in the earth by means of warmth, and out of it worms and other things are generated. An intelligent Artist will readily understand how great a variety of wonders is performed by Nature through this element, as a sperm, but the said sperm must be operated upon, having already within it an imagined astral seed of a certain weight. For Nature produces pure things by means of the first putrefaction, but things far purer by means of the second, as you see in the case of wood, where vegetable fibre is produced as the result of the first putrefaction, while the putrefaction of wood engenders worms and insects-natural forms endowed with sentient life; and it is clear that animate creatures endowed with sense and motion belong to a higher creative level, and are moulded of a purer substance than plants.

Water is the menstruum (solvent) of the world, and exists in three degrees of excellence: the pure, the purer, and the purest. Of its purest substance the heavens were created; of that which is less pure the atmospheric air was formed; that which is simply pure remains in its proper sphere, where, by the Will of God, and the co-operation of Nature, it is guardian of all subtle substances here below. It has its centre in the heart of the sea; its polar axis coincides with that of the earth, whence flow forth all springs and fountains of water, which are presently swollen into great rivers. This constant movement of water preserves the earth from combustion, and distributes the seeds of things throughout its length and breadth. Yet all water courses return to the heart of the sea. As to the ultimate fate of this water opinions are divided. Some say that all water is generated in the stars, and the sea does not overflow its shores because the water is consumed by fire as it reaches the heart of the sea. But this hypothesis is contrary to Nature's methods of working: Nature produces like out of like -and how can the stars, which are air and fire, produce water? Moreover, the safety of this earth depends on the equilibrium of the four elements; if at any time the total quantity of one element exceeded that of the others, the universe would relapse into chaos. Hence, if the stars generated water, they must manifestly produce an equal quantity not only of air and fire, but also of earth-which is manifestly absurd. It is much more reasonable to suppose that the waters are chained down, as it were, to the foundation of the earth by the circumambient air, and that they are constrained by it to continue in a ceaseless movement towards the Arctic pole-because no vacuum is possible in Nature; which is also the reason why there is a Gehennal fire in the centre of the earth, which is presided over by the Archeus (the first principle) of Nature. For in the creation of the world God first of all separated the quintessence of the elements from the weltering mass of chaos; and out of it He evolved fire, the purest of all substances, giving to it the most exalted place in the universe, and making it, in a special manner, the dwelling-place of His Sacred Majesty. In the centre of chaos was kindled that fire which afterwards distilled and carried upward the purest substance of water But because this most pure fire now occupies the firmament, and surrounds the throne of God, the waters have been condensed into a body beneath it; and thus the sky is formed, while the water which now forms the atmospheric air and the lower firmament is due to the action of a lower and grosser fire As the water of the firmament cannot pass the bounds of that highest and celestial fire, so the lower fire cannot pass through the atmospheric air to the earth; nor can the air pass the bounds of this lower fire The water and the earth were formed together into one organic mass Only one part of this water was volatilized into air, in order to protect the earth from the fierce and consuming heat of the sun If there had been a vacuum in the air, all the water would have evaporated; but as the space below the firmament is already filled up with air, the great bulk of the water is kept below, near the centre of the earth, by the pressure of the air These natural conditions continue to operate day by day, and through their normal action the world will be preserved from destruction during the good pleasure of the Creator. The central fire is kindled day by day by the universal motion and influence of the celestial bodies. This fire heats the water and a certain quantity of the water is dissolved into air; the air day by day keeps down by its weight the residue of the water, and causes it to form one mass with the earth And as the equilibrium of the world is thus naturally preserved by the Creator, so every natural generative process in the world must repeat the same conditions on a small scale. Thus the elements below act in perfect unison with the elements above, which God created of a far greater purity and excellence, and the example of obedience to their influences, which is set by the whole universe, is imitated on a small scale by the constituent parts of the world below. But let us now proceed to explain the flux and reflux of water. There are two Poles-the Arctic Pole in the north, and the Antarctic Pole, or the southernmost point of the earth The Arctic Pole possesses the property of magnetic attraction; the Antarctic Pole that of magnetic repulsion. Thus the Arctic Pole attracts the waters along its axis, and then they are again repelled by the Antarctic Pole along its axis; and, as the air does not permit inequality, they are once more forced back to their centre, the Arctic Pole In this their continual course from the Arctic to the Antarctic Pole, they pass through the middle (i.e., along the axis) of the earth, are diffused through its pores, and break out here and there as springs and fountains, which are swollen into rivers, and return to the Point whence they first flowed forth This universal motion is incessantly proceeding The waters then, are not generated by the stars and consumed in the heart of the sea; but they flow forth from the centre of the sea into the whole earth, and are diffused through all its pores On this principle the Sages have constructed conduits and aqueducts since it is well known that water cannot rise higher than the level of its spring or fount If this were not an actual fact, art would vainly found its practical conclusions upon it; and the natural principle involved is illustrated in the process by means of which wine is drawn out of a cask.

It may be objected to our view that if the water of our springs were derived from the sea, it would be salt, and not sweet, as we actually find it to be The answer to this objection lies in the fact that the sea water, in its passage through the pores of the earth, gradually deposits all the salt which it contains, and thus wells forth from the ground in a sweet and fresh condition It should, however, be remembered that some of our springs-called mineral or saline springs-actually do exhibit all the original saltness of the sea water which has not passed through earth calculated to retain its mineral element In some places we also meet with hot springs, which are caused by the passage of the water through certain spots where large deposits of sulphur have been set afire by the central heat of the earth; every one who has tasted this water must have observed its sulphureous flavour Something closely analogous happens when the water passes through large deposits of iron, or alum! or copper, and acquires their taste Thus the earth IS a great distilling vessel, formed by the hand of an all wise Creator, on the model of which all Sages have constructed their small distilling vessels; and if it pleased God to extinguish the central fire, or to destroy) the cunning machinery, this universal frame would relapse into chaos. At the end of time, He will kindle the Central Fire into a brighter flame, will cause all the water to evaporate, will calcine the earth-and thus the earth and the water will be rendered more subtle and pure, and will form a new and more glorious earth The operations of the earth and the water are always performed in combination, and are mutually dependent, since they are the two tangible elements, in which the other two work invisibly. Fire keeps the earth from being submerged, or dissolved; air keeps the fire from being extinguished; water preserves the earth from combustion. This is what the Sages call the equilibrium of the elements, and it illustrates the aid which they render to each other. Fire is closely associated with earth, and air with water. It will suffice if we remember that elementary water is the sperm and menstruum of the world, and the receptacle of seed.

CONCERNING ELEMENTARY AIR

The most noble element of air is inwardly heavy, visible, and fixed, outwardly light, volatile, and invisible. It is hot and moist, Is tempered by fire, and is nobler than earth or water. Air is volatile, but may be fixed, and when fixed, renders all bodies penetrable. Its purest substance has been formed into the vital spirits of animals, that which is less pure into the circumambient atmosphere, and the grosser residue has remained in the water, and associates with it as fire with its kindred earth. In the air the seed of all things is formed, as it were, in the body of the male, and is projected by its circulative motion into its sperm, which is water. It contains the vital spirit of all creatures, is the life of all, and penetrates and forces its seed upon all, as the man does upon the woman. It nourishes, impregnates, conserves the other elements; and we are taught by daily experience that it is the life not only of minerals, animals, and vegetables, but also of the other elements. We see that water becomes foul and unwholesome without a supply of fresh air; without it fire is extinguished-as is well known to Alchemists who regulate the temperature of their fire by the supply of air. Air is also that which conserves the pores of the earth. In short, the whole universe is kept fresh and sweet by air, and it is the vital element of man, beast, plant, and stone. It contains the seed of all things which is forced up, into vegetables for instance, through the pores of the earth by the action of fire, and thus the tree is built up atom by atom out of the vital element of congealed air. This vital force has remained in it ever since the time when the Spirit of Life brooded over the waters in the air. The magnetic power of life which air undoubtedly possesses, was put into it by God at the Creation. As the magnet attracts to itself hard steel, and as the Arctic Pole attracts to itself the water, so the air, by means of the vegetable magnet which is in the seed, draws to itself the nutriment of the menstruum of the world (which is water). This power of attracting water is in a certain part (viz., the 280th part) of all seed. If, then, any one would be a cunning planter of trees, he should take care to turn the point of attraction towards the North; for as the Arctic Pole attracts water, so the vertical point draws to itself the seminal substance. If you would know what the point of attraction in a tree is, submerge it entirely in water; that point which always appears first, will be the point of attraction. In the air, then, is the seed and the vital spirit, or abode of the soul of every creature.

CONCERNING ELEMENTARY FIRE

Fire is the purest and noblest of all elements, full of adhesive unctuous corrosiveness, penetrant, digestive, inwardly invisible, fixed, hot and dry, outwardly visible, and tempered by the earth. Of its purest substance was created the Throne of the Almighty; of that which is less pure, the Angels; out of fire of an inferior purity were created the stars and the heavenly luminaries; that which was less pure still was used to bear up the heavens; that which is impure and unctuous -- that, namely, which we have termed the fire of Gehenna -- is in the centre of the earth, and was there inclosed and shut up to set this lower world in motion. Though these different fires are separate, yet they are also joined together by natural sympathy.

This element is the most passive of all, and resembles a chariot when it is drawn it moves; when it is not drawn, it stands still. It exists imperceptibly in all things; and of it is fashioned the vital rational soul, which distinguishes man from all other animals, and makes him like God. This rational soul was divinely infused into his vital spirit by God, and entitles him to be regarded as a microcosm, or small world by himself. But the fire which surrounds the Throne of God is of an infinitely pure and simple essence, and this is the reason that no impure soul can know God, and that no human eye can penetrate this essential fire, for fire is the death and destruction of everything composite-and all material substances are of this nature What I said about the restful passivity of fire, applies in a certain sense to the eternal calm and unchangeableness of the Divine Nature. For as the fire sleeps in the flint, until it is roused and stirred up from without, so the power of God, which is a consuming fire, is only roused to action by the kindling breath of His Almighty Will. How calmly and solemnly does not even an earthly monarch sit enthroned in the pomp and state of his royalty! His courtiers hardly venture to move, and all around is calm and still. But when he rises what a stir of motion and activity does he not cause! All that are about him arise with him, and presently you see him sweeping along in grand and stately majesty. Yet the pomp of an earthly prince is but a faint reflex of the glory of the King of Kings. When He utters the voice of His Will, all heaven is roused, the world trembles, and thousands of angels speed forth on His errand. But it may be asked how I come to have this knowledge about heavenly things which are removed far beyond human ken. My answer is that the Sages have been taught of God that this natural world is only an image and material copy of a heavenly and spiritual pattern: that the very existence of this world is based upon the reality of its celestial archetype; and that God has created it in imitation of the spiritual and invisible universe, in order that men might be the better enabled to comprehend His heavenly teaching, and the wonders of His absolute and ineffable power and wisdom. Thus the Sage sees heaven reflected in Nature as in a mirror . and he pursues this Art, not for the sake of gold or silver, but for the love of the knowledge which it reveals; he jealously conceals it from the sinner and the scornful, lest the mysteries of heaven should be laid bare to the vulgar gaze. If you will but rightly consider it, you yourself are an image of God, and a little picture of the great world. For a firmament you have the quintessence of the four elements attracted to the formative womb out of the chaos of seed, and bounded by your skin; your blood is fire in which lives your soul, the king of your little universe) acting through the medium of the vital spirit; your heart is the earth, where the Central Fire is always at work; our mouth is your Arctic, and your stomach your Antarctic Pole, and all your members correspond to some part of the greater world as I have set forth at some length in my work on the Harmony of the Universe and in the Chapter on Astronomy. In the microcosm of man's nature the soul is the deputy or Viceroy of the Creator. It governs the mind, and the mind governs the body: the mind is conscious of all that is conceived in the soul, and all the members understand the mind, obey it, and wait eagerly to carry out its behests. The body knows nothing of itself; all its motions and desires are caused by the mind; it is to the mind what the tool is to the craftsman. But though the rational soul operates in the body, a more important part of its activity is exerted on things outside the body: it rules absolutely outside the body, and therein differs from the vital spirits of brute beasts. In the same way, the Creator of the world partly acts in and through things belonging to this world, and is thereby, in a sense, included in this world. But He absolutely transcends this world by that infinite part of His activity which lies beyond the bounds of the universe, and which is too high and glorious for the body of the world. The great difference between the soul's extracorporal, and God's extramundane, activity, is that man's rational activity is purely imaginative and mental, whereas God's thoughts are immediately translated into real existences. I might be mentally in the streets of Rome, but my journey would

THE NEW CHEMICAL LIGHT

be purely imaginative; God's conceptions are at once objective essences. God, then, is included in the world, only as the soul is enclosed in the body, while it has power to do things which far transcend the capacity of the body. By material relations such as these you may know God, and learn to distinguish Him from the material manifestations of His power. When once the gates of knowledge have been flung wide for you, your understanding will be enlarged.

We said that fire was the quietest of all elements, and that it is stirred by a kind of motion well known to the Sages. The Sage should be perfectly acquainted with the generation and destruction of all things; he is familiar with the creation of the heavens, and the composition and commixtion of things terrestrial; yet, though he knows everything, he cannot make everything. He knows the anatomy and composition of the human body-yet he cannot make a man. This is a mystery which the Creator has kept in His own hand. Nature cannot work till it has been supplied with a material: the first matter is furnished by God, the second matter by the Sage. But in the philosophical work Nature must excite the fire which God has enclosed in the centre of each thing. The excitation of this fire is performed by the will of Nature, and sometimes also by the will of a skillful Artist who can dispose Nature, for fire naturally purifies every species of impurity.

All composite substances are purified by fire, as all substances that are not fixed owe their purification to water It is the property of fire to separate and divide composite substances; and this separation means a purging away of the impure from the pure. This element also acts secretly, by marvellous means, not only in opposition to the rest of the elements, but also to all other things For as the reasonable soul was made of this most pure fire, so the vegetable soul was made of the elementary fire which Nature governs The fire which is contained in the centre of any given thing acts in the following way Nature provides the motive power, which stirs up the air; the air stirs up and rouses the fire, which separates, purges, digests, colours, and brings every seed to maturity, and expels the matured seed through the sperm into places or wombs, either pure or impure, more or less hot, dry, or humid; and according to the nature of the place or womb, different things are produced (cp. the Twelve Treatises). So the Most High God has ordained that, in the economy of the universe, one thing should be at enmity with another, and that the death of one thing should be the life of the other; that one thing should consume what another produces, and evolve out of it some higher and nobler form of life. The elementary separation of all living things is death; and hence it is necessary for man to die, as his body is compounded of the four elements, which cannot hold together for ever. In spite of this fact, our science furnishes an incontestible proof of man's original immortality. It is certainly true that all composite substances are liable to decomposition; that this decomposition, when it takes place in the animal world, is called death; and that the human body is a substance compounded of the four elements. But it is also true that the elements of Paradise, where man was created, are not subject to this law, seeing that they are most sure and incorruptible heavenly essences, and if man had remained in this pure and celestial region, his body would have been incapable of natural decay. Adam, however, in an evil day for our race, disobeyed his Creator, and straightway was driven forth to the beasts, into the world of corruptible elements which God had created for the beasts only. From that day forward his food was derived from perishable substances, and death began to work in his members. The pure elements of his creation were gradually mingled and infected with the corruptible elements of the outer world, and thus his body became more and more gross, and liable, through its grossness, to natural decay and death. The process of degeneration was, of course, slow in the case of Adam and his first descendants; but, as time went on, the seed out of which men were generated became more and more infected with perishable elements. The continued use of corruptible food rendered their bodies more and more gross-and human life was soon shortened to a very brief span indeed. In some favoured climes, where men eat and drink moderately, they still sometimes live to a green old age; but in our latitudes men abridge the term of their natural existence by grossly filling themselves with an excess of elementary corruptible food, and thus, before their time, become like "the beasts that perish." When the pure and essential elements are joined together in loving equilibrium, as they are in our Stone, they are inseparable and immortal, like the human body in Paradise; whence also our philosophical treasure has been compared to the creation of man, an analogy which modern wise men, who take all things literally, have understood as referring to the corrupted generation of this present order, which is produced from corruptible elements.

It was the recollection of man's immortality in Paradise that first set Sages a-thinking whether those pure and essential elements might not be obtained in this world, and united in one body. At length a merciful Creator made known to them that the desired conjunction of such elements existed in gold. It could not be found among the animals who are sustained by corruptible food, nor in vegetables, because they exhibit the elements in a state of inequality and contention. When corruptible elements are united in a certain subject, their strife must sooner or later bring about its decomposition, which is, of course, followed by putrefaction; in putrefaction, the impure is separated from the pure: and if the pure elements are then once more joined together by the action of natural heat, a much nobler and higher form of life is produced. In the strife of the elements, which follows when a body has been broken up by the victory of water, earth and air unite with fire, and together they overcome the water, digest, cook, and ultimately congeal it—which is the beginning of a new life. For if the hidden central fire, which during life was in a state of passivity, obtain the mastery, it attracts to itself all the pure elements, which are thus separated from the impure, and form the nucleus of a far purer form of life. It is thus that our Sages are able to produce immortal things, particularly by decomposition of minerals; and you see that the whole process, from beginning to end, is the work of fire.

Thus, then, we have briefly set forth as much as will serve our purpose concerning the four elements. Truly the description of each might be extended into a large volume, but we postpone all amplification for our Treatise on Harmony, which, God helping, if our life be spared, will be opportune to a more large discourse upon natural things.

CONCERNING THE THREE PRINCIPLES OF ALL THINGS

The three Principles of things are produced out of the four elements in the following manner: Nature, whose power is in her obedience to the Will of God, ordained from the very beginning, that the four elements should incessantly act on one another, so, in obedience to her behest, fire began to act on air, and produced Sulphur; air acted on water and produced Mercury; water, by its action on earth, produced Salt. Earth, alone, having nothing to act upon, did not produce anything, but became the nurse, or womb, of these three Principles. We designedly speak of three Principles; for though the Ancients mention only two, it is clear that they omitted the third (Salt), not from ignorance, but from a desire to lead the uninitiated astray. Whoever would be a student of this sacred science must know the marks whereby these three Principles are to be recognised, and also the process by which they are developed. For as the three Principles are produced out of four, so they, in their turn, must produce two, a male and a female; and these two must produce an incorruptible one, in which are exhibited the four (elements) in a highly purified and digested condition, and with their mutual strife hushed in unending peace and goodwill. In every natural composition these three represent the body, the spirit, and the hidden soul; and if, after purging them well, you join them together they must, by a natural process, result in a most pure substance. For though the soul is most noble, yet it cannot reach the goal without the spirit which is its place and abode; and if it is your desire to bring it back to a given place. both the soul and the place must be purged and washed from all impurity, so that the soul may dwell in glory, and nevermore depart. Without these three Principles, the Artist can do nothing, since even Nature is powerless without them. They are in all things, and without them there is nothing in the world, neither, indeed, can be. Their origin being such as we have described, it is from these, by an imitation of Nature, that you must produce the Mercury of the Philosophers, and their first matter, bearing in mind the laws which govern natural things, and especially metals. Do not think that Salt is unimportant because it is omitted by the Ancients; they could not do without it, even if they did not name it, seeing that it is the Key which opens the infernal prison house, where sulphur lies in bonds. The three Principles are necessary because they are the immediate substance of metals. The remoter substance of metals is the four elements, but no one can produce anything out of them but God; and even God makes nothing of them but these three Principles Why, then, should the Sage lose time and labour over the four cements, when he has the substance made ready to his hand by Nature ? It is surely less troublesome to go three miles than four, and as these three Principles exist in all things. and, according to their proportions, etc., produce either metals, or plants or animals, it is best to use them as our first substance. The body is earth, the spirit water, the soul fire or sulphur of gold. The Spirit augments the quantity of the body, the soul the virtue. But because in the matter of weight there is more of spirit than of fire, the spirit is uplifted, oppresses the fire, and attracts it to itself in such a way that both augment in virtue, and the earth, which is mediate between them, augments in weight. The Artist should determine which of the three Principles he is seeking and should assist it so that it may overcome its contrary. Afterwards he must seek by his skill to supplement what has been wanting in Nature and thus his chosen Principle will obtain the necessary victory. The element of earth is nothing but a receptacle, in which fire and air carry on their strife through the mediation of air. If water predominate, temporal and corruptible things are produced; if fire obtains the victory, it produces lasting and incorruptible things. So you know which of the elements ought to receive your aid. Moreover, though fire and water are in all things, they can produce nothing without air and earth. Their activity is aroused by external heat (in Nature, the Central Fire of the earth), and in their struggle they are assisted each by that which is like to it. By this strife they are subtilized in the pores of the earth, and when they ascend to the surface they produce flowers and fruit, in which they closely associate together as friends; and the more they are subtilized and purified in their ascent, the more excellent are the fruits which they produce.

When the purification has thus been performed, let water and fire become friends, which they will readily do in their earth which ascends with them; and the process will be the more speedily and perfectly accomplished, if you combine the two in their proper proportions-thus improving upon Nature In all natural compounds fire is always the smallest part; but it is aided and stirred up by the action of outward fire; and according as fire is overcome or obtains the mastery. imperfect or perfect things are the result. The outward fire does not enter into the composition as an essential part of it, but only by the effect which it helps to produce. The inward fire is sufficient, if it only receive nutriment from the outward fire, which feeds it as wood feeds elemental fire; in proportion to the quantity of nutriment the inward fire grows and multiplies. Care should be taken, therefore) that the outward fire is not so fierce as to devour instead of feeding, the inward fire. Gentle coction will be the best means of attaining perfection, and of adding excellence to weight But as it is difficult to add to a compound substance, I would advise rather to produce the same effect by removing that which is present in an excessive quantity. Remove that which is too much, and let the compound develop itself naturally. But many artists sow straw instead of grain; others sow both; many throw away that which the Sages love; others begin and do not persevere to the end; they look for short and easy labour in a difficult Art. But we say that this Art consists in an even mingling of the virtues of the elements-in the natural equilibrium of the hot, the dry, the cold, and the moist-in the conjunction of the male and female, the female having engendered the male, i.e., of fire and the radical humour of the metals. If you understand that the Mercury of the Sages contains within itself its own good Sulphur, digested and matured by Nature, you can accomplish the whole process by means of Mercury alone; but if you know how to add the supplement which our Art requires to the natural proportions of substances, to double the Mercury, and to triple the Sulphur, you will all the more quickly produce, first the good, then the better, and finally the best-though only one sulphur appears, and two mercuries (which, are, however, of the same stock); they should not be crude nor too much digested, yet well purged and dissolved (if you understand me).

It is really unnecessary to describe the matter of the Mercury and the Sulphur of the Sages, as it has already been as plainly delineated by the Ancients as is consistent with our vow. We do not altogether say that the Mercury of the Philosophers is a common thing, or that they have openly called it by its name, and that the matter from which Mercury and Sulphur are philosophically extracted has been plainly pointed out. For the Mercury itself is not found above ground, but is extracted by an artifice from Sulphur and Mercury conjoined, in short, Sulphur and Mercury are the ore of our quicksilver, and this quicksilver has power to dissolve, mortify, and revive metals, which power it has received from the sulphur (which has Some of the properties of an acid). In order to put you on the right track, I will also tell you the difference between our quicksilver and common mercury. Common mercury does not dissolve gold and silver so as to amalgamate with them; but when our quicksilver dissolves gold and silver, it almagamates with them in inseparable union, as water is mixed with water. Common mercury has bad combustible sulphur, which turns it black; our quicksilver contains incombustible, fixed, good, snow-white and red sulphur. Common mercury is cold and humid; our quicksilver is hot and humid. Common mercury blackens other bodies; our quicksilver renders them white and pure as crystal. Common mercury is changed by precipitation into a yellow powder and bad sulphur; our quicksilver is converted by heat into snow-white, good, fixed, and fusible sulphur. Common mercury becomes more fusible, our quicksilver more fixed, the more it is subjected to coction. Our quicksilver possesses such marvellous virtue that it would by itself be sufficient for our purpose, if subjected to gentle coction; but in order to accelerate its congelation, the Sages add to it its well digested and matured sulphur.

We might well have cited philosophers in confirmation of the points of our discourse, but as our writings are more clear than are theirs, we have no need of their support.

Whosoever understands them will understand us better. If you would practise our Art, learn first to hold your tongue, and <u>study the nature of minerals, metals, and vegetables.</u> Our Mercury may be obtained from all things, as everything has it; only from some substances it is more easily procured than from others. Our Art is not a matter of luck or accident, but is founded on a real knowledge, and there is only one matter in the world by which, and of which, the Stone of the Philosophers is prepared. The substance is indeed to be found everywhere, but the method of its extraction out of some matters would take a lifetime, and if you begin your search without a due knowledge of natural things, more especially in minerals, you will be working in the dark and in blindness. It is, indeed, possible to set about our Art in a casual manner; and some who actually operate on our quicksilver, begin at the wrong end, and thus fail in bringing it to perfection, because they are quite in the dark about its real nature. Yet after all, we must confess that a right knowledge of our Art is the gift of God alone, and is granted to diligent students in answer to earnest and importunate prayer. To the Master it may appear easy enough; but to the beginner it must seem at first very hard and uphill work. He should not, however, despair, for in due time he will receive the reward of his diligence and aspiration; even in the dangers which the knowledge may bring upon him, he will be kept from harm by the loving hand of Providence, as I can testify from personal experience. We have with us God's Ark of the Covenant, which contains the most precious of earthly things, and is guarded by the holy Angel of the Lord. We heard that our enemies had fallen into the snare which they had laid for us; that those who sought our lives had been enclosed in the meshes of death; that those w ho attempted to rob us of our goods had lost all that they possessed; and that those who strove to blacken our reputation, died in shame and dishonour. Such is the care which God has of us, Who, from our childhood, has kept us safe under the shadow of His wings. And the feeling uppermost in our minds is the humbling consciousness of our utter unworthiness: we do not deserve the very least of His great mercies. But one thing we do and will] do: our hope and trust always have been, are, and will be, in Him alone. We will not put our confidence in men or in princes: we will place ourselves in the hands of One who remains unchanged when all earthly power and greatness have passed away. The fear of the Lord is the beginning of wisdom: never did Sage utter truer word than this; and if we would attain to the knowledge of this glorious science, if we would be able to use it well when we possess it, we must wait on God continually. and importune Him with earnest prayer. But to proceed with our description of the Matter. We said that it was quicksilver, and quicksilver only: whatever is added, is gained from this same substance. We have repeatedly affirmed that all things earthly are evolved out of three principles. But for our purpose they must be purged of their impurities, and then recombined; that which is wanting is added-and thus imitating and assisting Nature we arrive at a degree of perfection such as Nature is unable to attain, on account of the impurities with which her operations are clogged. Do not suffer yourself to be confounded by the apparent contradictions which the Sages have introduced into their writings for the purpose of keeping their secret. Select only those sayings which are agreeable to Nature; take the roses, leave the thorns. If you wish to produce a metal, your fundamental substance should be metallic; only a dog can beget a dog; without wheat you will vainly plough your field; and all your endeavours in this Art will be in vain, unless you take your radical humour from a metal. There is one substance, one Art, one operation It is as erroneous to suppose that any of the particular benefits of our Stone can be enjoyed before the Stone itself has been prepared, as it would be absurd to imagine that you can have a branch without a root or tree. If you have water you can cook in it various kinds of meat, and thus obtain broth of different flavours; but there will be no broth unless you have both the water and the meat In metals, then, as in all other things, there is only one first substance, but the universal substance is modified in a vast variety of ways, according to the course of its subsequent development. Thus one thing is the mother of all things. This great fact ought always to be borne in mind in studying the works of the Sages; for nothing but mistakes and disappointment can result from a slavishly literal interpretation of their books. It is a pity that, instead of humbly studying and following Nature our Alchemists are so ready to adopt any fancy or notion that happens to pass through their minds. They seek to attain the end not only without a middle part, but without so much as a beginning. But how can anyone who sets about our Art in so casual and haphazard a manner expect anything but disappointments? Let our Alchemists have done, then, once for all, with their sophistical methods, to which they ascribe so great an importance-with their dealbations, rubrefactions, fixations of the Moon, extractions of the soul of gold,-and let them place themselves under the unerring guidance of Nature For though the soul of the metal has to be extracted, it must not be killed in the operation; and the extraction of the living soul, which has to be reunited to the glorified body, must be carried on in a way very different from the violent method commonly prevailing among Alchemists. We do not propose to multiply wheat without seed corn. But let us, in concluding this part of the subject, earnestly inculcate on the student's mind the necessity of having seed that will germinate and grow, and to avoid the use of seed which has been killed by an excess of fiery heat.

CONCERNING SULPHUR

Among the three principles the Sages have justly assigned the first place to Sulphur, as the whole Art is concerned with the manner of its preparation. Sulphur is of three chief kinds: that which tinges or colours; that which congeals mercury and essential sulphur, which matures it. The properties and preparation of this Sulphur we propose to describe, not in a set treatise, but in a dialogue like that which brought out the essential properties of Mercury. We will only say, by way of preface, that Sulphur is more mature than the other principles, and that Mercury cannot be coagulated without it. The aim and object of our Art is to elicit from metals that Sulphur by means of which the Mercury of the Sages is, in the veins of the earth, congealed into silver and gold; in this operation the Sulphur acts the part of the male, and our Mercury that of the female. Of the composition and action of these two are engendered the Mercuries of the Philosophers.

In our former dialogue we gave an account of the meeting of Alchemists, which a sudden tempest brought to so abrupt a close Among those who took a prominent part in the proceedings, was a good friend of the first Alchemist; he was not a bad man, or an impostor, but, as they say, nobody's enemy except his own; yet he was foolish withal, and though really very ignorant, had no small opinion of his own wisdom and learning. He had at the meeting been the foremost champion of the claims of Sulphur to be-regarded as the first substance of the Stone, and was satisfied that he would have been able to make good that claim, if the meeting had not been prematurely broken up. So when he got home he resumed his operations on Sulphur in a very confident spirit. He subjected it to distillation, sublimation, calcination, fixation, and to countless other chemical processes, in which he spent much time and money. without arriving at any result whatsoever. His failures at length began to prey on his health and spirits, and in order to recruit the former, and raise the latter, he fell into the habit of taking long walks in the neighbourhood of the town where he lived. But wherever he went he could think of nothing but Sulphur. One day, with his mind full of this besetting idea, and being wrought almost to an ecstacy he entered a certain verdant grove, in which there was abundance not only of trees, herbs, and fruits, but also of animals, birds, minerals, and metals. Of water there was indeed a great scarcity; it was carried to the place by means of aqueducts, and among these was a conduit flowing with water extracted from the rays of the moon ; -- but this water was reserved for the use of the Nymph of the grove. In the grove there were two young men tending oxen and rams, and from them he learned that the grove belonged to the Nymph Venus. The Alchemist was gratified enough, but all his thoughts were absorbed by the subject of Sulphur, and when he remembered the words of the Sages, who say that the substance is vile and common, and its treatment easy, when he recollected the vast amount of time, labour, and money which he had vainly spent upon it, he lifted up his voice and in the bitterness of his heart, cursed Sulphur. Now Sulphur was in that grove, though the Alchemist did not know it. But suddenly he heard a voice which said: "my friend why do you curse Sulphur? "

He looked up in bewilderment nobody was to be seen. "My friend, why are you so sad?" continued the voice.

ALCHEMIST: Master, I seek the Philosopher's Stone as one that hungers after bread.

VOICE: And why thus do you curse Sulphur?

ALCHEMIST: My Lord, the Sages call it the substance of the Stone; yet I have spent all my time and labour in vain upon it, and am well nigh reduced to despair.

VOICE: It is true that Sulphur is the true and chief substance of the Stone. Yet you curse it unjustly. For it lies heavily chained in a dark prison and cannot do as it would. Its hands and feet have been bound, and the doors of the dungeon closed upon it, at the bidding of its mother, Nature, who was angry with it for too readily obeying the summons of every Alchemist. It is now confined in such a perfect labyrinth of a prison, that it can be set free only by those Sages to whom Nature herself has entrusted the secret.

ALCHEMIST: Ah! miserable that I am, this is why he was unable to come to me! How very hard and unkind of the mother! When is he to be set at large again?

VOICE: That can only be by means of hard and persevering labour.

ALCHEMIST: Who are his gaolers?

VOICE: They are of his own kindred, but grievous tyrants.

ALCHEMIST: And who are you?

VOICE: I am the judge and the chief gaoler, and my name is Saturn. Alchemist: Then Sulphur is detained in your prison?

VOICE: Yes; but I am not his keeper.

ALCHEMIST: What does he do in prison?

VOICE: Whatever his gaolers command. *Alchemist:* And what can he do?

VOICE: He can perform a thousand things, and is the heart of all. He can perfect metals and minerals, impart understanding to animals, produce flowers in herbs and trees, corrupt and perfect air; in short, he produces all the odours and paints all the colours in the world.

ALCHEMIST: Of what substance does he make the flowers?

VOICE: His guards furnish him with vessels and matter; Sulphur digests it; and according to the diversity of the digestion, and the weight of the matter, he produces choice flowers, having their special odours.

ALCHEMIST: Master, is he old?

VOICE: Know, friend, that Sulphur is the virtue of the world, and though Nature's second-born-yet the oldest of all things. To those who know him, however, he is as obedient as a little child. He is most easily recognised by the vital spirit in animals, the colour in metals, the odour in plants. Without his help his mother can do nothing.

ALCHEMIST: Is he the sole heir, or has he any brothers?

VOICE: He has some brothers who are quite unworthy of him; and a sister that he loves, and who is to him as a mother.

ALCHEMIST: Is he always the same?

VOICE: As to his nature, it is always the same. But in person his heart only is pure: his garments are spotted.

ALCHEMIST: Master, was he ever quite free?

VOICE: Yes; in the days of the great Masters and Sages whom Nature loved, and to whom she gave the keys of the prison.

ALCHEMIST: Who were these wise adepts?

VOICE: There have been very many, and among them Hermes, who was one and the same with the mother of Sulphur. After him there were kings, princes, a long line of Sages, including Aristotle and Avicenna. All these delivered Sulphur from his bonds.

ALCHEMIST: What does he give to them for delivering him?

VOICE: When he is set free, he binds his gaolers, and gives their three kingdoms to his deliverer. He also gives to him a magic mirror, in which the three parts of the wisdom of the whole world may be seen and known at a glance: and this mirror clearly exhibits the creation of the world, the influences of the celestial virtues on earthly things, and the way in which Nature composes substances by the regulation of heat. With its aid, men may at once understand the motion of the Sun and Moon, and that universal movement by which Nature herself is governed-also the various degrees of heat, cold, moisture, and dryness, and the virtues of herbs and of all other things. By its means the physician may at once, without consulting an herbarium, tell the exact composition of any given plant or medicinal herb. But now-a-days men are content to trust to the authority of great writers, and no longer attempt to use their own eyes. They quote Aristotle and Galen, as if there was not much more to be learned from the great Book of Nature which is spread open before them. Know that all things on the earth and under the earth are engendered and produced by the three principles, but sometimes by two, unto which the third, nevertheless, adheres. He who knows these three principles, and their proportions as conjoined by Nature, can tell easily by their greater or less coction, the degrees of heat in each subject, and whether they have been well, badly, or passably cooked. For those who know the three principles know also all vegetables by sight, taste, and odour, for these senses determine the three principles, and the degree of their decoction.

ALCHEMIST: Master, they say that Sulphur is a Medicine.

VOICE: Nay, you might rather call him a physician, and to him who delivers him out of prison, he gives his blood as a Medicine.

ALCHEMIST: How long can a man ward off death by means of this universal Medicine?

VOICE: Until the time originally appointed. But many Sages who did not take it with proper caution, have died before that time.

ALCHEMIST: Do you call it a poison then?

VOICE: Have you not observed that a great flame swallows up a small one? Men who had received the Art by the teachings of others, thought that the more powerful the dose they took of our Medicine the more beneficial would be the effect. They did not consider that one grain of it has strength to penetrate many thousand pounds of metals.

ALCHEMIST: How then should they have used it?

VOICE: They ought to have taken only so much as would have strengthened and nourished, without overwhelming, their natural heat.

ALCHEMIST: Master, I know how to make that Medicine.

VOICE: Blessed are you if you do! For the blood of Sulphur is that inward virtue and dryness which congeals quicksilver into gold and imparts health and perfection to all bodies. But the blood of Sulphur is obtained only by those who can deliver him from prison; and therefore he is so closely imprisoned that he can hardly breathe, lest he should come to the Palace of the King.

ALCHEMIST: Is he so closely imprisoned in all metals?

VOICE: In some his imprisonment is less strict than in others.

ALCHEMIST: Why, Lord, is he imprisoned in the metals so tyrannously?

VOICE: Because if he once came unto his royal palace, he would no longer fear his guards. He could look from the windows with freedom, and appear before the whole world, for he would be in his own kingdom, though not in that state of highest power whereto he desires to arrive. Alchemist: What is his food?

VOICE: His food is air, in a digested state, when he is free; but in prison he is compelled to consume it in a crude state.

ALCHEMIST: Master, cannot those quarrels between him and his gaolers be composed?

VOICE: Yes, by a wise and cunning craftsman.

ALCHEMIST: Why does he not offer them terms of peace?

VOICE: He cannot do so by himself: his indignation gets the better of his discretion.

ALCHEMIST: Why does he not do so through some commissary?

VOICE: He who could put an end to their strife would be a wise man, and worthy of undying honour. For if they were friends, they would help, instead of hindering each other, and bring forth immortal things.

ALCHEMIST: I will gladly undertake the duty of reconciling them. For I am a very learned man, and they could not resist my practical skill. I am a great Sage, and my Alchemistic treatment would quickly bring about the desired end. But tell me, is this the true Sulphur of the Sages?

VOICE: He is Sulphur; you ought to know whether he is the Sulphur of the Sages.

ALCHEMIST: If I find his prison, shall I be able to deliver him?

VOICE: Yes, if you are wise enough to do so. It is easier to deliver him than to find his prison.

ALCHEMIST: When I do find him, shall I be able to make him into the Philosopher's Stone?

VOICE: I am no prophet. But if you follow his mother's advice, and dissolve the Sulphur you will have the Stone.

ALCHEMIST: In what substance is this Sulphur to be found?

VOICE: In all substances. All things in the world -- metals, herbs, trees, animals, stones, are its ore.

ALCHEMIST: But out of what sub stances do the Sages procure it?

VOICE: My friend, you press me somewhat too closely. But I may say that though it is every where, yet it has certain palaces where the Sages can most conveniently find it; and they worship it when it swims in its sea and sports with Vulcan (god of fire), though there it is disguised in a most poor garb. Now is it in a dark prison, hidden from sight. But it is one only subject, and if you cannot find it at home you will scarcely do so in the forest. Yet, to give you some heart in your research, I will solemnly assure you that it is most perfect in gold and silver-most easily obtained in quicksilver.

With these words Saturn departed, and the Alchemist, being weary with walking, fell into a deep sleep, in which he saw the following vision: He beheld in that grove a spring of water, near which Salt and Sulphur were walking and quarreling, until at last they began to fight. Salt dealt Sulphur a grevious wound, out of which there flowed, instead of blood, pure, milk-white water, that swelled into a great river. In this river the virgin goddess, Diana, came to bathe; and a certain bold prince, who was passing by, was inflamed with great love towards her; which she, perceiving and returning, pretended to be sinking under water. The prince bade his attendants assist her; but they excused themselves, saying that the river, though it looked small and all but dried up, was most dangerous. " And," said they, ' many of those who have passed here before have perished in it." Then that prince threw off his thick cloak, plunged into the river, and stretched out his arm to save the beautiful Diana; but she grasped it so convulsively that they both sank under water together. Soon afterwards their souls were seen rising upward above the water, and they said, " We have done well, for in no other way could we be delivered from our stained and spotted bodies."

ALCHEMIST: (speaking): Will you ever return into those bodies?

SOULS: Not while they are so polluted-but when they are cleansed, and the river is dried up by the heat of the sun.

ALCHEMIST: What do you do in the meantime?

SOULS: We soar above the water till the storm and the mists cease.... Then the Alchemist thought that he saw a great number of his fellows come to the spot where the body of the Sulphur lay slain by the Salt; and they divided it among themselves, and gave a piece to him also. Then they went home, and began to operate on their (dead) Sulphur, and are at it to this day. Presently Saturn returned, and the Alchemist said: Master, come quickly, I have found Sulphur -- help me to make the Stone.

SATURN: Gladly, my friend. Prepare the quicksilver, and the sulphur, and give me the vessel.

ALCHEMIST: Oh, I do not want Mercury. It is a delusion and a snare, as my friend the other Alchemist discovered to his smart.

SATURN: I can do nothing without quicksilver.

ALCHEMIST: Oh no, we will make it of Sulphur only.

So they set to work on that piece of dead Sulphur, and sublimed, calcined, and subjected it to all manner of chemical operations. But they produced nothing save little bits of sulphurous tow, such as they use for lighting fires. Then the Alchemist confessed the fruitlessness of his endeavours, and bade Saturn set about the work in his own way. Then Saturn took two kinds of quicksilver, of different substance but one root, washed them with his urine, and called them the sulphurs of sulphurs; then he mixed the fixed with the volatile, after which he placed them in a proper vessel, and set a watch to prevent the sulphur from escaping; afterwards he placed them in a bath of very gentle heat -- and thus they made the Philosopher's Stone, which must always follow as the outcome of the right substance. Then the Alchemist took it in his hand, admired its beautiful purple colour, and danced about with it, shouting aloud with joy and delight. Suddenly the glass slipped out of his hand and broke into a thousand pieces; the stone vanished; and the Alchemist awoke with nothing in his hand but some pieces of sulphurous tow. There are a good many Alchemists who, having an extremely favourable opinion of themselves, and fancying that they can hear the grass grow, rail against this Art, because they think that if the Stone were not a mere delusion, they could not have failed to find it. We, for our part, are not over anxious to rob these people of their comfortable conviction. But to men who were worthy (men both of high and low degree) we have repeatedly proved the reality of our Art by incontestable ocular evidence. Let me warn those who wish to follow the true method in studying our Art, airways to read with constant reference to natural facts, and never, under any circumstances, to do anything contrary to Nature If the Sages say that fire does not burn, they must not believe it; for Nature is greater than the Sages; but if they say that it is the property of fire to dry and heat things, they will accept this statement, because it is in accordance with the truth of Nature --- and the facts of Nature are always simple and plain. If any one came and taught you to make this Stone, as though he were giving you a receipt for making cheese out of milk, he might speak more plainly than I have done; but I am compelled to veil and conceal my meaning because of the vow which my Master exacted of me.

My last words shall be addressed to you who have already made some progress in this Art. Have you been where the bridegroom has been married to the bride, and the nuptials were celebrated in the house of Nature? Have you heard how the vulgar have seen this Sulphur, as much as have you who have taken such pains to seek it? If you wish that even old women should practise your philosophy, shew the dealbation of these sulphurs, and say openly to the common people: Behold, the water is divided, and the Sulphur has gone forth; when it returns it will be whiter than snow, and will congeal the water. Burn the Sulphur with incombustible sulphur, wash it, and make it white and purple until the Sulphur becomes Mercury, and the Mercury Sulphur, and you can proceed to quicken it with the soul of gold. Our Mercury must be corrected by means of Sulphur-otherwise it is unprofitable. A prince without a people is a wretched sight-and so is an Alchemist without Sulphur and Mercury. If you understand me, I have spoken.

The Alchemist went home, bewailed the broken Stone, and his folly in not asking Saturn about the Salt of the Sages, and the way of distinguishing between it and ordinary salt. The rest he related to his wife.

Conclusion Every student of this Art should first carefully read what is said-in this and other Treatises -- about the creation, operation, properties, and effects of the four elements; otherwise he cannot apprehend the nature of the three principles, or find the substance of the Stone, or understand its development. God has created the elements out of chaos; nature has evolved the three principles out of the elements; and out of these principles she makes all things, and gives power to her beloved disciples to produce marvelous preparations. If Nature produces metals out of the principles, Art must follow her example. It is one of the rules of Nature to act through intermediate substances; and this book should enable the student to judge what substances are intermediate between the elements and metals, and between meals and the Stone. The difference between gold and water is great, that between water and mercury not so great, and that between gold and mercury very small, for mercury is the habitation of gold, water the habitation of mercury, and sulphur is that which coagulates mercury. The whole arcanum lies hidden in the Sulphur of the Sages, which is also contained its the inmost part of their Mercury, which has to be prepared in a certain way that shall be described on another occasion.

I have not written this Treatise with the object of refuting the ancient Sages, but only for the purpose of correcting, explaining, and supplementing their statements. After all, they were only men and they sometimes did make assertions which can now no longer be maintained. For instance, when Albertus Magnus says that gold was once found to have developed in the teeth of a dead man, he is out of harmony with the possibilities of Nature; for an animal substance can never develop into a mineral. It is true that animals and vegetables contain sulphur and mercury, as well as minerals; but these principles are animal and vegetable, not mineral. If there were no animal sulphur in man, the mercury of his blood could not be congealed into flesh and bones; and if plants contained no vegetable sulphur, their mercury or water (sap) would not be congealed into leaves and flowers. The three kinds of sulphur are essentially the same, but, like the three mercuries, they are differentiated according to the three kingdoms, and cannot act outside their own kingdoms. Each kind of mercury can be coagulated by none but its own sulphur, and if gold was found in the teeth of a dead man it must have been introduced in an artificial manner --- either as gold, or in the shape of some other metal which by the gradual action of its own metallic sulphur on its metallic mercury, was afterwards transmuted into gold. It is mistaken impressions and superstitious notions, like this one of Albertus Magnus, that we have set ourselves to correct in this Treatise, by stating once for all the true facts of animal, vegetable, and mineral development.

Let the painstaking student be satisfied to have received a true account of the origin of the Three Principles. There is no greater help towards a successful end than a good beginning. I have in this Treatise started the student on the right road, and given him clear and practical directions. With God's blessing, and by dint of diligent and persevering study, he may now fairly hope to reach the glorious goal. But I, having told out all that is lawful for me to utter, now commit myself to the mercy of a loving Creator, who will receive me to Himself; and I commend the gentle and pious Reader to the same great Father of All, to whom be praise and glory, through the endless succession of the ages.

HERMES [says]:

You must have a good knowledge of the True Principle of both Natural and Artificial Substances. For he who knows not the true First Principle will never attain to the end.

THE LOVE OF GOD AND OF YOUR NEIGHBOUR IS THE PERFECTION OF ALL WISDOM.

TO LOVE GOD IS THE HIGHEST WISDOM, AND TIME IS OUR POSSESSION.

UNTO HIM BE ALL HONOUR, PRAISE, AND GLORY

Made in the USA
Lexington, KY
02 September 2017